A GENIUS IN THE FAMILY

HIRAM STEVENS MAXIM

as he appeared at the time of these tales

Hiram Percy Maxim

A
GENIUS
IN THE FAMILY

SIR HIRAM STEVENS MAXIM
THROUGH A
SMALL SON'S EYES

A COMMON READER EDITION
THE AKADINE PRESS

A Genius in the Family

A COMMON READER EDITION published 1999
by The Akadine Press, Inc., by arrangement with HarperCollins Publishers
Inc., successors in business to Harper & Brothers Publishers.

A COMMON READER EDITION and fountain colophon are trademarks
of The Akadine Press, Inc.

ISBN 1-888173-63-7

10 9 8 7 6 5 4 3 2 1

TO MY SON

HIRAM HAMILTON MAXIM

WHO WILL APPRECIATE IT MORE THAN
ANYONE ELSE, THIS BOOK IS
AFFECTIONATELY DEDICATED

CONTENTS

CONTENTS

PUBLISHER'S NOTE

SO little is said in this book about the remarkable achievements for which its subject (to say nothing of its author) is famous that a word of reminder should be said.

Sir Hiram Stevens Maxim was not merely an extraordinary parent, but also an extraordinary scientific worker, one of the most brilliant and renowned engineers and inventors of his day. His international renown came chiefly from his invention of the Maxim gun, the first efficient automatic gun; but he also made a fundamental contribution to the development of the incandescent carbon lamp, and invented automatic gasgenerating plants, steam and vacuum pumps, engine governors, gas motors, automatic sprinkling apparatus, and numerous other useful devices.

Born in Maine in 1840, Maxim was a paragon of Yankee resourcefulness—and of Yankee eccentricity. He had less than five years of schooling in his entire life. In his youth he wandered about the eastern United States and Canada, taking odd jobs as carriage-painter, cabinet-maker, and mechanic, and meanwhile studying science and engineering furiously. By the time when this book opens (in the early 1870's) he was already a rising engineer and inventor with several inventions to his credit; a Brooklyn, New York, householder, occupied in New York chiefly with the development of machines for generating illuminating gas. In 1878 he became chief engineer of one of the first electric-lighting concerns in the country, the United States Electric Lighting Company. He narrowly missed being the acknowledged inventor of the incandescent lamp; in a patent suit Thomas A. Edison proved priority by only a matter of days.

He foresaw the automatic machine-gun, and designed and built the first of those millions of guns which were to be known the world over as Maxim guns. He offered this gun to the United States War and Navy Departments, both of which declined it on the ground that it was impractical—little more than an interesting and ingenious mechanical curiosity. This reception on the part of his fellow countrymen wounded him deeply and he took his gun to England and offered it to the British War Office, which took it up. Thenceforward Maxim lived in England, leaving his family in America. He formed the Maxim Gun Company, which in 1896 was merged with the English armament firm of Vickers to form Vickers Sons and Maxim (later Vickers, Ltd.). In the War of the Soudan his gun covered itself and its inventor with glory; at the battle of Omdurman it was one of the big factors in saving the day for the British. In 1900 he became a British subject; in 1901 he was knighted by Queen Victoria.

Meanwhile, during the 1890's—several years before the Wright brothers learned to fly—he had experimented with flying-machines and had built a huge steam-airplane that actually lifted itself from the ground, but was wrecked (the weight of the fuel and water which a steam-plane had to carry making it impracticable).

Sir Hiram retired from the Vickers firm in 1911, died in England in 1916.

His younger brother, Hudson Maxim, who is mentioned here and there in this book, was likewise a brilliant inventor, famous chiefly for his invention of smokeless powder.

Hiram Percy Maxim, the author of the book, was Sir Hiram Stevens Maxim's son (and Hudson Maxim's nephew). His varied scientific and engineering achievements carried on the family tradition, his best-known contribution being the Maxim silencer. He had completed the manuscript of the book and it had been accepted for publication when he was taken suddenly ill on a Western trip and died at La Junta, Colorado, on February 17, 1936.

[xi]

PREFACE

MOST of us men become fathers at one time or another. As far as my information goes, none of us has very much experience in the business when he embarks upon it. I am sure my father merely blundered into fatherhood without giving the matter any serious consideration. He gave every evidence of conceiving fatherhood to be a means provided by nature for perpetrating humorous misconceptions upon young and inexperienced offspring. As the first of these offspring I was the butt of a host of most amazing undertakings. From birth to the age of twelve, when my father went abroad, to remain permanently, as it turned out, I lived an utterly different sort of family life from that of any of my young friends. I am prepared to believe that no boy was ever brought up as I was. Having had no previous experience in being brought up, I was not conscious that there was anything unique about my situation, and it was not until after my father left the family and we gradually settled down to the conventional, that I realized what an unusual life we had been living.

It would be unfortunate, it has seemed to me, were the atmosphere of my father's house not recorded and made available, for I am persuaded that the examples of clever invention, amazing audacity, extraordinary humor, and passionate persistence of purpose (and heaven-born patience on the part of my mother) may be of interest outside the family. It is in this spirit that I present this intimate picture of the family life of my father, the late Sir Hiram Stevens Maxim, one of America's distinguished engineers and scientists.

HIRAM PERCY MAXIM.

A GENIUS IN THE FAMILY

PART I

THIRD STREET, BROOKLYN

I SUSPECT I had one of the most unusual fathers anybody ever had. I was his firstborn. He knew considerably less than nothing about children and he had to learn how to be a father. He learned on me.

He did not learn easily. In fact, as I look back upon it, he never thoroughly learned how to be a father. As for me, although I had no previous experience, I do not remember having very much difficulty in learning to be a son. I accepted my father as a general run-of-the-mine father; he wore trousers, had a deep voice and a beard, and otherwise looked like other fathers. When we first met he did not impress me particularly. Indeed, either he was so colorless or I was so unobserving that it was well over two years after we first met that I noticed he was a member of the family.

As the reader will discover, he was anything but colorless. I must have been unobserving, because I utterly failed to note the adding of such an important item to our family as my sister Florence. I distinctly remember when there were but three of us, my father, my mother, and myself; but to save my life I cannot remember the occasion of my sister's joining the family, although I was nearly four at the time. As for my second sister, who arrived two and a half years later, I remember her coming very clearly, as I had the impression the house had caught on fire.

My father saw to it very early in my life that there should be an erroneous impression in my mind concerning the words "papa" and "man." I was allowed to acquire the impression that the words were synonyms. On a certain occasion this led to a misunderstanding between me and the driver of a coal-truck. I happened to be out on the sidewalk in front of our house in Brooklyn, New York, when this driver delivered our coal. Shoveling the coal down the coal-hole was an interesting operation to me. I became impressed also with the evident importance of our family, because of the large amount of coal which we seemed to need. I spoke to the driver of the coal-truck on the subject, addressing him as "papa." It surprised him very much. He denied that he was a papa, was very positive that he was not my papa, and went so far as to state that he was not married. What being married had to do with it was not plain to me, and I maintained that because he wore trousers and had a mustache he must be a papa.

I am told that I added that most papas of my acquaintance did not have such dirty faces as his.

When the coal had all been put in this person took the matter up with my mother, stating that I had called him "papa." My mother explained to me after this little colloquy that I had only one papa, that he was not the driver of a coal-truck, but, instead, was the papa who lived with us.

Younger readers would do well to realize that in the days of which I write there were no telephones, no electric lights, no electric street cars, no bicycles, no automobiles, no skyscrapers, no radios, and no airplanes. To go anywhere one either walked or was hauled by a horse or a steam-locomotive. We were living on Third Street near Smith Street in Brooklyn at this time. Even in the large cities—and Brooklyn was one—the streets had a very small amount of traffic in them, except in downtown districts. No one ever thought of stop lights and traffic policemen. The average street car or wagon moved at about five miles per hour. No one ever thought of being run over and killed. The streets were clear and open. Indeed, there were very few overhead wires on poles, except in downtown New York. The streets were lighted with gas-lamps and men came around every evening on every street in the city and lighted them, and came again in the early morning and put them out.

[3]

The streets in many places were paved with rounded cobblestones. Probably there was not a rubber-tired vehicle in all the world. Had there been bicycles, they could not have been ridden in most city streets.

Our house on Third Street was a few doors from Smith Street. There was a horse-car line on Smith Street. In one direction it ran to Fulton Ferry, which, in my estimation, was a very long way off. My father went to his business in New York on the Fulton Ferry. In the other direction the Smith Street horse cars ran to Ninth Street, where they turned and crossed the Gowanus Canal, the water in which was indescribably dirty. I used to marvel that water could be so dirty.

Some distance beyond the canal the car line ran past the place where the snow plows were kept. I used to watch carefully for this place when I was taken to Prospect Park, because the gate in the fence would be open sometimes and I could see the snow plows. This vision used to thrill me to the marrow every time; snow plows were the most interesting things in my world. In the winter, when they would pass along Smith Street with a long string of horses pulling them, sweeping the snow off the tracks and blowing it all over everybody on the sidewalk, the spectacle rendered me speechless. The driver of the snow plow reminded me of Santa Claus. He had a very red face and he was always frosted all over with snow. He had a very loud voice and he used to shout at the horses and crack a long whip. Nothing fascinated me quite so much as the passage of the snow plow and I used to beg my father to talk about it.

My father had wandered down from the wilds of Maine, where he was born, and at the time of which I write, 1873, he was senior partner of the firm of Maxim & Welch, builders of steam-engines and gas-generating machines on Center Street, New York.

Our house on Third Street, Brooklyn, had a high stoop which led to the second floor, where were the parlor, living-room, and two of our bed-chambers. The dining-room, pantry, and kitchen were on the first floor, which was two or three steps below the ground level. They were entered by means of a basement door which was under the brownstone stoop. There was a front yard, which must have been very minute, and in which my mother attempted to coax a bit of sickly grass to grow. I was the cause of the grass being sickly. I was forever in difficulties because I was forbidden to walk upon this grass, and it seemed to me to be the one place where it was imperative that I should walk frequently.

Between the yard and the sidewalk of the street was a very ornate cast-iron fence. It had a gate in it which had to be swung open and closed with deliberation.

Being made of cast iron, it was heavy, and swinging it open and closing it took time. This gate stands out conspicuously in my memory because, being invariably in a hurry, as was also the case with my father, I could not resist the temptation, now and again, to postpone closing it. This always got me into trouble with my mother, who, I am sure, what between me and my father, must have lived a troubled life.

My father had a simple solution for the gate nuisance. It was to vault over it. Both going and coming he always vaulted it, unless he was burdened with packages. I used to envy him this ability, and I used to direct the attention of my little friends to the fact that my father was the only father on the street who jumped his gate. Business men in those days always wore high silk hats and Prince Albert coats. I believe we call them frock-coats today. It would be quite a spectacle in these times to see a gentleman in a silk hat and a frock coat vaulting his areaway fence.

§ 2

On the corner of our street was a drug store in the windows of which were large glass vessels containing highly colored liquids. All drug stores had these vessels of highly colored liquids in my day. Only very old-fashioned drug stores have them today. I was sent frequently to this drug store on simple errands.

The man in the drug store owned a little white dog. He was a very gentle little dog and he seemed to like me. We had no dog at our house. All we had was a very small baby which cried too much. One day I told the man in the drug store that I loved his little dog. I think I suggested to him that it would be very nice of him if he gave me the dog. Indeed, I suspect that I suggested it several times. The drug-store man became impatient finally and one day told me to go out and find a penny with a head on each side and bring it to him and he would give me the dog. This seemed a simple thing to do, so I hurried home to get one.

I found my mother and asked her to let me see all of her money. This seemed to astonish the dear lady. She asked me why. I told her that the man in the drug store promised to give me his little white dog if I would bring in a penny which had a head on each side. My mother smiled and explained to me that the man was joking, that every penny had a head on one side only, and that he made the offer only because he knew there was no such thing as a penny with a head on both sides. My mother was wasting her breath. There was the dog, and I wanted him, and all I had to do to own him was to find a penny with a head on both sides. My mother could not sense the importance of the matter. I insisted that we look over her pennies for one with a head on both sides.

I remember how we argued as we went upstairs to her bureau drawer, where she kept her purse, and how she emptied all of her coins out of the purse into her lap; and how I, standing at her knee, examined both sides of every penny; and how disappointed I was when I found that every one of them had a head on one side only. I was thwarted, but by no means defeated. I made up my mind that my problem was above a woman's head and that I would be obliged to seek my father's assistance. He was a man and I was very sure that he could find me a penny with a head on both sides, for he could do wonderful things.

The rest of the afternoon was spent waiting at the corner for him to arrive. He always came by horse car and I knew exactly where he would get off. After a very long wait he arrived. Running up to him, I asked him to look in his pockets and see if he had a penny with a head on both sides. Naturally he was astonished, but instead of showing his surprise and treating me as though I were a little child, he pretended to take the matter seriously. Stopping on the sidewalk and handing me his evening paper and a package to hold, he fished out of his pocket all the coins he had, and selecting the pennies, we went carefully over each one, looking to see if any of them had a head on both sides. They all had a head on one side only. He professed surprise at this and he went over them again in order to be sure. This encouraged me, for obviously he had expected to find one. Evidently they were to be had, which was precisely the impression he wished to convey to me.

As he gathered up his paper and package he asked me casually what I wanted the penny for. I told him that the man in the drug store had said that I could have his little white dog if I would bring in a penny with a head on both sides. "Well," said my father, "that ought to be easy. When I go over to New York tomorrow I will see if I can find one. They must have plenty of them over there."

I was very much elated. I knew my father would have no trouble with a little matter like this. He could do anything, and if he said he would bring me a penny with a head on both sides he would do it, which meant that the little white dog would be mine. When he left for New York the next morning I was careful to remind him about the penny. He assured me he would not forget.

It was a very long day. I thought late afternoon would never come. I had made up my mind just where

I was going to have the little dog sleep, where he was going to have his meals, and what we were going to do together. In the meanwhile a very busy man in New York, with heavy responsibilities resting upon his shoulders, went into his factory tool-room, put a penny in a lathe and faced off the "tail" side of it until it was just half the thickness of a normal penny. Then he repeated the operation with another penny, which gave him two half pennies. He then soldered these two thin half pennies together, thereby producing a coin of normal thickness but with a *head on both sides.* When the edge had been burnished the joint could not be seen, whereupon he probably smiled and placed the unique coin in his pocket.

That afternoon I was at the corner, waiting for him. When he arrived I ran out to greet him and asked him if he had found the penny. Acting as though he had forgotten the matter, but that on a chance shot he might have one among his other coins, he reached into his pocket and drew them out. There were several pennies, and looking at each one, he picked out one which had a head on both sides. Handing it to me, he asked if that was what I was looking for. I was none too familiar with the heads and tails matter and I had to compare the double-headed one with the others in order to make up my mind. With his assistance it became clear that this penny had a real head on each side. I was for going and getting the dog forthwith, but my father suggested that we go home first, and then after supper he would go up to the drug store with me.

I can see my mother now, as we three sat at the table, she astounded at the double-headed penny, utterly unable to account for it, but knowing it was a trick, while my father laughed at her, for there the penny was, and it certainly had two heads on it. Knowing my father as she did, and as I came to know him in due time, she must have said what I heard her say many hundreds of times in later years, "Now, Hiram, please don't do anything foolish and in bad taste." This all went over my head. I recall my inability to understand her attitude. There was the penny, staring everybody in the face with its two heads. Why all the talk? The double-headed penny assured getting the dog. What possible objection could my mother have to the proceeding?

After supper my father and I sauntered up to the drug store. As we entered, I dancing with joyous anticipation, my father hung back. Running up to the man, I held out to him my double-headed penny and told him I had come for the dog. The man took the penny, turned it over and over and over again, stared at me, glanced at my father in a sheepish sort of way, and gave every evidence of being taken thoroughly aback. I suppose that this little scene was what my father had been looking forward to all day. The drug-store man asked me where I had obtained the penny. I told him that my father had given it to me. This involved the latter, who then stepped forward, asking what the difficulty seemed to be, and acting as though he had no previous knowledge of the matter. The drug-store man held out the penny in a helpless sort of way, saying something about a joke. My father, acting as though he could not understand, took the penny, glanced at it casually, and handed it back, saying something about not remembering having seen one like it before.

I asked if I was going to get the dog. To my complete dismay, the drug-store man indicated that I was not. I remember the maze of confusing talk, which did not interest me, for it was the dog that I wanted. My father did not put as much value on the dog as did I. He appeared to be involved in the legal aspects of the case. After a lot of talking, during which I thought him particularly stupid, because he knew perfectly the original terms of the bargain between me and the drug-store man, he appeared to discover for the first time that the proposition had been that if I brought in a penny with a head on both sides I would get the dog. Having established this fact, my father summed up the difficulty. It appeared to him I had been offered a certain dog in consideration of my bringing in a penny with a head on both sides. It appeared to him I had done this. It appeared to him it was up to the drug-store man to fulfill his part of the bargain. In other words, if the bargain between me and the drug-store man was what both sides agreed it was, then there was but one solution, and that was for the drug-store man to hand over the little white dog. Of course the drug-store man had not the slightest intention of giving up the dog. When this had become established my father made it plain that it would be more prudent if the drug-store man would be careful about making offers in the future, unless he proposed to live up to them. Where that poor drug-store proprietor thought we had got the double-headed penny was never disclosed.

We took our double-headed penny home. I was very much disappointed. I had believed the drug-store man, and I fairly pined for that little dog. It was my first contact with a broken pledge. I had not known before that there was such a thing in the world as a broken pledge. My father did not take my view of the matter. He had had his little joke; the drug-store man had been given the surprise of his life and had been placed in an embarrassing position. That was all there was to it. The incident was closed.

§ 3

With my father, one never knew what was going to happen from one moment to the next. On one occasion he and I were walking through an uptown street in New York after dark. In those days Fifty-eighth Street was far uptown. We probably were walking through Fifty-eighth Street from one avenue to another. There were any number of house lots which had not yet been built upon. These lots had board fences to prevent passers-by from falling into the rock pit which most of the vacant places seemed to be. In front of one of these board fences, and in the very dim light of the infrequent gas lamps, a tough-looking specimen demanded money. It really amounted to a hold-up, although no pistol was involved.

My father was an extraordinarily powerful man and as quick as a cat. Before the man had finished speaking my father grabbed him and actually boosted him up on top of the fence and pushed him over. What he fell into on the other side, how much he was hurt, how he got out, and what he thought had happened to him have filled me with wonder these many years. My father was the last man on earth to start monkeying with.

One of our many cooks at Third Street was an Irish girl. One day a man came to the door and told her that he was taking orders for photograph enlargements. If she would let him have one of her photographs he would enlarge it, put it in a beautiful frame, and bring it back in a few days. The price was only two dollars, which was less than the cost of the frame as he represented matters. He exhibited a beautiful frame in which was an excellent enlargement of a cabinet-size photograph of a young woman. Our cook yielded, gave him one of her photographs and two dollars. As might be expected, the man never sent any enlargement. After several weeks had passed my mother told my father of the fraud. To everybody's complete surprise he became very indignant, scolded the girl, and evinced a deep resentment against the man who would thus prey upon servant girls. He cross-examined her and gathered all the information she could give him, and for several Sundays after that he and I pursued the trail of the photograph man.

After he had run down a great many addresses in Brooklyn and found that the man had moved on, the trail led to the stockyards in Jersey City. After securing another address at these stockyards my father noticed that the cattle in the pens crowded toward him whenever he moved about. This seemed a curious thing, and he went from pen to pen, experimenting, the cattle crowding toward him in every case. Something led him to suspect that the animals were thirsty. To prove it he opened a valve in a pipe leading to a trough in one of the pens. As soon as the water began to flow a terrible stampede developed among the cattle in that and in neighboring pens. They became crazed at the sound of the water and fought desperately for a place at the trough. It terrified me because they seemed very large beasts and very angry, and I feared they might break down the fence in their fighting and get out.

My father then went to other pens and opened the water-valves, and the thirsty animals behaved the same way there, too. His indignation over this new situation diverted him from the pursuit of the photograph man.

He was busy opening valves when a watchman came hurrying up. I knew there was going to be a scene and I dreaded what I knew was to come. Sure enough, my father pitched into the watchman, demanding to know when the cattle had last been watered. The poor watchman realized he was dealing with a man who meant business and explained that it was orders from the office that the cattle should not be watered after Thursday morning, so that when they came to be sold by weight on Monday they would drink enormous quantities of water and weigh more. This was too much, and my father delivered himself of a few well-chosen and very pointed remarks about such inhuman practices, warning the watchman that he would report the matter to the proper authorities the first thing Monday morning. It was impossible for him to water all the cattle in the stockyards, so after more very acid remarks about the persons who operated the stockyards we departed and resumed our search for the photograph man.

We finally located the swindler. He turned out to be a barber in the most wretched barber shop I have ever seen. My father recovered the two dollars obtained from our cook, and had the man arrested and fined. As for the cattle, my father did just what he said he would do, and I am under the impression that he went to great lengths in the matter, giving a lot of his time to it, and being instrumental in having some kind of law passed in New Jersey prohibiting this form of cruelty.

§ 4

While I am on the subject of cooks I am reminded of an especially hectic Sunday morning with one of them. My father used to pretend to be overcome by the stupidity of the average cook or housemaid. We came to have a series of stupids. I remember Stupid the Fifth very distinctly. I thought this was her real name. Everybody, my mother excepted, called her by that name.

It was one of the several stupids who was the unwitting subject of one of his so-called "experiments" one Sunday morning in the kitchen. The kitchen is no place for the head of the family. I learned that very early in life. In my family I naturally keep out of the kitchen if it is possible to do so. Not so my father. He loved the kitchen, and I came to learn never to leave his side when he was in it. There was likely to be action at any minute.

He had been reading that the sensation of extreme cold is the same as that of extreme heat. It occurred to him one Sunday morning to demonstrate it. He secured two stove pokers, hooked affairs which were used in those days to poke the ashes out of a coal fire in the open grates we had. One of these pokers he placed in a bath of snow mixed with alcohol. The alcohol melts the snow and produces a liquid which may have a temperature considerably below zero. The other poker he placed in the open grate in the kitchen range. When it was red hot he walked around the kitchen with it, and used it to burn a bit of wood and create an odor of something burning. While all this stage play was going on the Irishwoman was busy preparing the Sunday dinner. Unconsciously she became aware of the presence of a red-hot poker. As I look back at it, I marvel at the perfection of the man's psychology.

When he had paraded the red-hot poker around the kitchen for some time, and had told me (in a voice which he intended the cook to overhear), how red-hot irons were used to brand cattle on their necks, and how it must hurt, he went outside and got the cold poker, which he wiped off and secreted under his coat. Returning to the kitchen, he withdrew from the open grate of the kitchen range the other poker, which was at a brilliant red heat. Grasping this red-hot poker, and dancing about as though it were so hot that even the handle burned him, he stepped up to the cook from behind, waved the red-hot poker where she could see it and feel its heat, pulled it back, drew the cold poker from under his coat and clapped the latter against the cook's neck, shouting, "LOOK OUT!" and emitting a loud hissing sound.

Naturally, the poor woman thought he had branded her on the neck with a red-hot poker. I saw the entire proceeding and knew that he did nothing of the kind. The cook gave a piercing scream, clapped the corner of her apron to her neck, and fell fainting into a chair. My mother, convinced that some dreadful accident had occurred, came running from upstairs, to find my father in fits of laughter and the cook emitting periodic screams as she came out of her faint.

My poor mother was distraught. The screams shattered her nerves as they did mine. She tried desperately to get the cook's hand down from her neck in order to ascertain the extent of her injury, but the cook evidently thought she would bleed to death if she removed her hand and the apron. This nerve-racking scene went on for some time, the cook letting go a piercing scream every so often. After a great amount of effort my mother succeeded in getting the woman's hand down from her neck, and the surprising fact was disclosed that there was not even a mark visible, which threw my mother into complete confusion. She was very excitable and for some time she and my father and the cook shouted at cross purposes at one another, nobody listening to anybody else and nobody being able to make head or tail of what the others were talking about. My father saw that he must have gone too far, and did his best to explain that it was an experiment he had been conducting, that nobody had been hurt, and that it was all very funny if only the others would see it in that light; and besides, things had come to a pretty pass if a man could not experiment in his own house.

The cook could not be persuaded to see the matter in that light, insisting that she had been branded on the neck with a red-hot poker, although a look in the mirror failed to disclose even a slight mark. She threw up her job then and there, declaring that she would not remain with a family where the man of the house branded the servants on their necks. My mother had a flood of tears, the cook packed up her belongings and departed in high dudgeon, and the Sunday dinner was late and a very doleful affair.

§ 5

On another Sunday morning my father called to me and asked if I had noticed that every Sunday morning the policeman on the beat spent an hour or so in the areaway of the house across the street. I had noticed it and I had also noticed that the housemaid of the people opposite was involved in these Sunday-morning visits. My father asked me what I imagined could be the trouble over there that they had to call the police every Sunday morning. I was old enough at the time to sense that the policeman was not there to straighten out any trouble or to protect anybody; he was there because the housemaid was there. I had on two or three occasions heard my father use the word "sparking," although he had not realized that I had noticed it; so I suggested that perhaps the policeman was sparking the housemaid. My father was amazed at my knowledge, for I was only five, and he repeated the word after me. "Sparking?" Then, unable to resist the temptation, he continued,

"What do they do when they spark?" I could see the little lines around his eyes and I knew that I had interested him.

My father pretended to be concerned about the sparking business. We watched the policeman and the maid, and finally he said: "I tell you what we ought to do, Percy. We ought to make them stop that sparking every Sunday morning. If they spark on Sundays, how do we know that they will not spark on other days; and we cannot have this policeman spending his time sparking when he should be watching for bad people."

There seemed a certain virtue in this point of view, and with the directness of the child I asked how we could stop them. Said he: "Of course we can't go over there and tell them to stop sparking; but I tell you what we could do. We could get a bean-blower and blow beans at them."

I inquired what he meant.

"Well, I'll tell you," said he. "Between now and next Sunday I shall bring over from New York a long brass tube that will be nice and straight. It will be just big enough on the inside to accept a bean. Then we can get some beans from Mamma and we can blow them over there and make him stop sparking the housemaid."

This seemed most irregular to me; but no matter if it **was** irregular or not, if he was going to do it, it would be interesting. So I gave my whole-hearted support to the plan. I recall how funny he looked, even to me, when he cautioned me not to tell Mamma about it because she would not understand. He was absolutely right. I knew that Mamma would not understand.

When the next Sunday came around I had forgotten about the sparking business. But my father had not. When my mother had disappeared upstairs for the morning he laid aside a drawing he was working on and, calling me, pointed across the street, remarking something to the effect that they were at it again. That reminded me and I hastened to ask him if he had remembered to bring the brass tube for the beans. He said he had the tube in the closet where we kept our umbrellas. There followed a pause, so I asked him why he did not get it out and blow some beans. He seemed to have been waiting for me to suggest this, which struck me as being very odd. I probably suggested that while he was getting the brass tube I would ask Mamma for some beans. He vetoed this idea instantly. He would get the beans. Mamma ought not be disturbed. And it needed a certain kind of bean which only he knew how to select. I saw the wisdom of this procedure, for I could see that to ask my mother for beans would raise the question of what the beans were wanted for; and something told me that she would not give her whole-hearted support to using them to blow at a policeman.

After much shifting of things and adjusting of the window curtain we were ready to blow our first bean. I was very much excited, for I had not the slightest notion in the world what the bean was supposed to do after it had been blown. To my surprise, my father pointed the bean-blowing tube at the top of the building across the street. Putting his mouth to the tube, he sent a little white bean across the street where it struck the building about three stories up, directly over the areaway where the policeman and the housemaid were sparking. The bean bounced off the wall of the building and fell vertically into the entrance into the areaway. Nothing happened, so my father blew another. It also fell into the areaway. It seemed to me to be a most curious way to go about "smoking out" a policeman. But I was wrong.

After half a dozen beans had been blown against the wall and had fallen into the areaway, the policeman came out and looked very hard at the windows over his head. Then it was that I saw and appreciated my father's strategy. By blowing the beans against the wall and high up, my father made them appear to the policeman to be coming from overhead. Probably the very last place he would have expected to find the beans coming from was across the street. He peered at all the windows, waiting for the unknown one upstairs to throw another bean, so he could catch him at it. But nothing came, my father being too clever to blow while the policeman was looking up. Presently he went down into the area again, which was the signal for a perfect fusilade of beans. Out the policeman popped again, this time walking out on to the sidewalk in order to gain a better view of the windows above. I suppose if some innocent person had selected this moment to raise a window and look out, nothing on earth would have convinced the policeman this person was not guilty of blowing the beans.

But nobody raised a window, so the mystified policeman had nothing else to do but to return to the areaway and the housemaid. He had no more than entered when the beans rained down again. This time he dashed out, thinking to be so quick that he would catch the blower. But there was somebody quicker than he was. He had not a chance in the world. He walked around this time in a most determined manner, my father in the meantime rolling around in gales of merriment. I remember that I thought it was a good joke, but that—like all my father's jokes—it was not entirely above criticism. It seemed to me to be playing with fire, this making a policeman the butt of a joke.

[25]

The policeman finally had to give up and return to the areaway and the housemaid. The instant his figure disappeared into the areaway another downfall of beans took place. He did not pop out so quickly this time. When he did come out he waved good-by to somebody in the areaway, doubtless the housemaid, and came directly over to our side of the street. I thought he had detected us and I became alarmed. I suspect my father had a bit of a turn, because he rushed to the umbrella-closet with the tube and the beans, and when he returned pretended to be hard at work on his drawing. However, the policeman had come across the street in order to obtain a good view of all the windows in the house opposite. He stopped directly in front of our window, not fifteen feet from my father and me, and waited several minutes. Little did that policeman suspect that directly behind him were a man, a boy, a bean-blower, and a supply of beans.

We broke up that morning's sparking and we broke up several other sessions. Finally the policeman had to give up and do his sparking at other times. He never found out where the beans came from.

§ 6

A certain incident in our life on Third Street is very vivid in my memory, probably because of the fuss my mother made over it. It was something which she had to piece together, bit by bit, before she had the whole story.

We had among our friends a married couple of about my parents' age. Their name was Righter. The Righters were very "high church." My father, as might be imagined, was not "high church." He used to go to church occasionally with my mother to hear Henry Ward Beecher preach; but my mother said that she had to give up taking him because, unless the sermon was unusually interesting, he would yawn so much, sigh so loud, squirm in his seat so continuously, and stare so hard at the people in the near-by pews, that it made her fidgety. She finally had to give up trying to soak a little religion into him.

The Righters had me in frequently, not having any children of their own, and probably finding a little boy interesting. Mrs. Righter conceived it her duty to assist in my religious education, and so she used to teach me verses from the Bible. My mother kept this condition of affairs from my father, because she well knew that it would be most unsafe to let him in on any religious matters. But one day, like a child, I inadvertently let the cat out of the bag. In one of the fascinating philosophical discussions with which I was sometimes favored by my father, something was said about what should and what should not be done on a Sunday. I must have been between four and five years old at the time. Probably I asked why it was that things which might be done all right on Saturday afternoon were not proper on Sunday morning. Anything of this sort was irresistible to my father. He led me on until the word "Sabbath" crept into the discussion. I realized for the first time that it meant the same thing as Sunday.

That reminded me of my latest accomplishment, the result of Mrs. Righter's efforts; so I said to my father that we always should remember the Sabbath and keep it holy.

I shall never forget the look of amazement which swept over his face. Coming straight out of the blue from a little child of four, it must have been startling. When he had caught his breath the conversation continued something like this, according to family legend:

"Who told you that?"

"Mrs. Righter told me that's what everybody should do."

"Are you sure you have it the way Mrs. Righter told you to say it?"

"Yes. That's the way she says it."

"Just say it again, so I can try to find what is wrong about it, because I am sure you have it wrong."

"Remember the Sabbath and keep it holy."

"Well! I am surprised."

"What's the matter with it?"

"She told you wrong. Nobody who knows says it that way. I am surprised that Mrs. Righter should have told you the wrong way."

"Well—what is the right way?"

"The way I always say it is, 'Remember the Sabbath and go fishing.' "

"Go *fishing*?"

"Yes. You see, Percy, the fish always bite better on the Sabbath and people do not have to go to their business on that day, so, as you know, when you and I have gone fishing we always have gone on Sunday. We never went on any other day, did we?"

He was absolutely right. He always was right. He had taken me fishing down near Coney Island in a river and we had caught a lot of crabs, and it was on a Sunday. It had to be on a Sunday because, as he said, he had to go to his business every other day.

"Remember the Sabbath and go fishing," I repeated, wondering at the wide difference between what Mrs. Righter had told me and my father's version.

"That's right. Now you have it. That's the way everybody says it. You ought to tell Mrs. Righter the right way to say it, because she probably does not know about it."

I resolved to do it quickly, which was precisely what my incorrigible father planned.

It is a very curious thing what one remembers. I can distinctly remember climbing up the stairs in the Righters' house soon after this discussion. I remember that the stairs were carpeted and that the steps were very high for my short legs. I called to Mrs. Righter from downstairs and she called back to me to come along up. I must have begun my announcement to her when only part way up, for there is a clear picture in my mind of holding on to the banisters to help mount the high steps as I began telling her my father had said she had told me wrong about what to say.

"Told you wrong, Percy?"

"Yes, Mrs. Righter. My Papa says you told me wrong. The right way to say it is 'Remember the Sabbath and go fishing.'"

Something went wrong at this point. I did not know what it was, but I could see that Mrs. Righter was very serious. She said something in a very solemn voice which I took to mean that she was cross with me. This led me to cut my visit short. I went home. I was depressed. Mrs. Righter had never spoken to me that way before. There was only one person to whom I wanted to go—my mother.

She saw, quickly enough, that something was wrong,

as mothers have a way of doing. She asked me why I had returned from Mrs. Righter's so quickly. I did not want to discuss the question. It was too painful. But by degrees she aroused in me an argumentative mood, not a difficult thing to do with a Maxim. I assumed the offensive myself. I asked her what day it was that Papa and I went fishing. This appeared to surprise her more than ever. She replied that she could not remember, and what in the world had that to do with Mrs. Righter's being cross with me? I asked her if it was Sunday. She recalled that it must have been on a Sunday, because Papa always went to his business in New York on the other days. This clinched the matter with me. My father was right. We *had* gone fishing on Sunday. There was no other day when we could have gone. "Remember the Sabbath and go fishing" must be right. Mrs. Righter was wrong.

Convinced that I had the best of the argument, I told my mother that Mrs. Righter had told me wrong and that Papa had told me the right way to say it.

"*Say it!*" exclaimed my mother. "Say what?"

"Remember the Sabbath and go fishing," I replied.

The dear lady was aghast. Drawing me to her, she became very serious.

"What was it you said to Mrs. Righter, Percy? Tell Mamma exactly what you said."

[31]

"I told her that she told me the wrong way to say it. My Papa knew and he said the right way to say it was 'Remember the Sabbath and go fishing,' and," I added by way of convincing her, "that's right, because Papa and I do go fishing on Sunday, don't we Mamma?"

My poor mother! She saw the entire picture. It was considered, in those days, wicked to go fishing on Sunday. The fishing we had done was done secretly, so far as our neighbors were concerned. Here was a pretty how-d'-do. I recall nothing more about the incident. I have a vague memory of a tearful scene with my father over the Righter affair and some kind of coolness concerning the Righters. My mother patched up matters, but I am sure my father became *persona non grata* with the Righters, and I know that I did not enjoy going there as much as I had.

PART II

WE MOVED to Fanwood, New Jersey, in the spring of 1875. My father used to come out from New York on Saturday afternoons and remain with us until Monday morning. It was very much "out in the country" for us. It seems to me, as I look back upon it, that our house was miles out from the railroad station; but my uncle Frank and I walked the distance many times, so in reality I suppose it was half a mile or less. We had a horse and carriage, a barn, a pig, some chickens, a cow, a garden, a blackberry patch, and a hired man. My sixth birthday was on September 2, 1875, and my birthday present was to be taken to school for the first time. This enables me to establish the date of the incidents I am about to describe, and my own age. We had been in Fanwood some time before I went to school, so that I must have been only five years old when many of the events happened.

With the exception of my father, we were city-bred people. My father had been born and reared in the country near Sangerville, Maine. While he took no specific responsibilities for our amateur agricultural activities, nevertheless he made suggestions and acted in a consulting capacity. My mother decided that the house needed painting soon after we became settled, and it was decided to make use of this opportunity to bring down from Maine my uncle Frank, my father's youngest brother, then a young man in his twenties.

Uncle Frank was a particularly handsome young fellow, with wavy black hair, dark eyes, and a wonderful complexion. Like all the rest of the breed, he was remarkably profane. However, his profanity, like my father's, was never vulgar. Indeed, it was never ordinary profanity. Instead, it was a very real flow of soul. It was poetic; it had rhythm. My father was circumspect in his language before us children, but when he thought none of us were around he would give expression to some very wonderful sentiments. Young as I was, I realized that the words they used were exquisitely chosen. I listened to them entranced when by some good luck I happened to overhear one of their outbursts. It affected me in the same manner that splendid music affects me today. Their profanity had spaciousness, was commanding, had a strong dramatic flavor.

Hudson Maxim, another uncle, whom I came to know very intimately in later life, had this poetically profane gift in a particularly highly developed form. In recent times at his home at Landing, Lake Hopatcong,

New Jersey, he was showing my wife and me and our
son Hamilton a certain painting of which he was very
proud. He jostled another small painting which was
hanging higher up, and it fell and hit him on the head
on its way to the floor. It was only a moderate bump,
but the principle of the thing aroused him. Addressing
my wife, because she happened to be standing very close
beside him, he apostrophized Heaven, consigned to ever-
lasting fire the inspired idiot who hung the picture,
wished damnation upon the person who had selected
the wire and hooks by which the picture had been hung,
expressed his profound wonderment that his brains had
not been knocked out, and then went on with his story
about the first painting. It was profanity, and it startled
my wife no end, because she had never heard anything
like it before; but it was poetry, also.

Returning to Fanwood and my uncle Frank: He
seems to have been given the job of painting our house.
There were two colors on the clapboards, those above
a certain point being one color and those below this
point being another color. Uncle Frank was particularly anxious to finish the job by the time his brother
arrived from New York on Saturday afternoon. He had
worked very hard indeed in order to finish it on time.
Some half-hour before it was time for my father to
arrive, he had finished, and he removed the ladders,

paint-pots, and things, and cleared up generally. When all was done—and he was immensely pleased that he had been able to finish it—he and I walked out to the road to note the general effect. The first glance disclosed the ghastly fact that he had put the dark paint one clapboard too low on the end of the house. The end of the house, in short, did not match the front.

Uncle Frank was stunned. In a deep, resonant, ringing and very carrying voice that would have resounded in the largest theater and must have been heard all over the neighborhood, he called upon the Almighty to look down and explain how, on this beautiful afternoon, He could have found it in His heart to permit such a thing as this to happen. He submitted that it was a most damnable example of injustice wreaked upon an innocent and well-meaning man who had done his level best to finish the job before his brother Hiram arrived from New York. Why had he been permitted to go on and finish it without one thing being done to apprise him that he was doing it wrong?

After he had been going on in this strain for a few minutes my mother came to the window to find out what the loud talking was all about. As she listened and realized the magnitude of the flow of blasphemy, she became horrified and retired precipitately from the window. Next, our Irish cook burst out of a side door and ran out into the garden, where she stopped and stuck her fingers in her ears. She told me afterward that she ran out because she was afraid to stay in the house for fear it would be struck by lightning, notwithstanding there was a perfectly clear sky overhead. She assured me that with such swearing going on it was very dangerous to stay in a house. Next, my poor mother hurried out of the front door, evidently with the intention of interceding with Uncle Frank, but before she could reach him she was stricken. Poor dear, profanity, dog fights, and violence in general always made her ill. It was at this interesting juncture that James drove my father into the front yard.

The spectacle presented to his astonished gaze staggered even him. There was his brother Frank standing in the middle of the front lawn delivering an argument to the Almighty concerning the freshly painted clapboards; there was his wife not feeling at all well on the front lawn; there was his small son standing close to the orator, gazing up into the latter's face, fascinated and drinking in every word; and there was the servant girl standing out in the garden, terror written all over her face and a finger stuck in each ear.

My father asked to be informed what in the world was going on. When it was conveyed to him that Uncle Frank had painted one row of clapboards too low on the end of the house and was blaming it upon the Almighty, he calmed down Frank and brought the scene to an end. It was too bad, but while the scene lasted it was magnificent.

§ 2

We had what I considered a large body of water on our property. It was located on the edge of a growth of trees which I regarded as a great forest. I suppose it was a small grove of trees and that the "body of water" was a pool some forty or fifty feet in diameter. It was big enough to contain frogs and turtles and was about knee deep in the deepest place. I regarded it as a young ocean.

One Sunday my father wondered if it might not be good fun to build a raft. He had to explain to me what a raft was. He said that one put a lot of pieces of wood in the water, fastened them together, stood upon them, and went sailing around. This impressed me as being a very excellent idea indeed. No doubt I suggested that we ought to make one right away. I could not imagine anything that would be more wonderful than to go sailing around our pond. At five, one does not know that anticipation is much better than realization.

My father fell in with the notion. Together, he doing all the work and I asking all the questions, we built a raft, placing a box on it on which I was supposed to sit. A pole was cut to push the raft around. I was disappointed when the raft was finished. It seemed to me to be very ragged looking. Its top, where I was to stand, seemed dangerously low in the water. In fact it was just awash, which did not inspire me with confidence. Everything seemed very wet when we got it in the water. All things considered, it was not a prepossessing craft, and to venture to sea upon it appeared to me a most foolhardy undertaking. The entire enterprise lost its attractions and when it came to the trial trip I dared not venture upon it. This precipitated an unforeseen dilemma. I had asked for the raft, my father had worked very hard building it, and now, when it was all done and ready to try, I declined to get on it.

He argued with me and I fully recognized the soundness of his position. Nevertheless, it seemed to me that it was my life which was at stake, and not his. Nothing was said about his getting on the raft. Somehow, my mother, the hired man, the servant girl, and my little sister Florence had all been attracted to the pond to see me take a sail, and what had started out to be a little matter between me and my father had grown into a major family ceremony in which I was to play the stellar rôle. My declination to get on the raft brought the entire program to a stop.

I resisted until the tears threatened, which I knew I must control at all hazards, because my father was extremely unpleasant when I cried. Somehow, he got me on the raft and my mother, not wholly in sympathy with the proceedings, urged me to go along and get it over with. This attitude on her part, and the fact that she was near at hand, exercised a powerful influence, for I knew that she would not see any harm come to me. I am very sure that had she not been present I would have resisted embarking upon the pond on the crazy raft with the last ounce of strength I possessed.

My mother being present and mildly consenting, I allowed myself to be pushed on to the miserable thing, struggling mightily to hold back the tears. I was frightened at the novelty of the idea more than anything else, because, after all, standing upon a piece of wood which was resting on the land at one end was not so alarming. But presently it began to move as my father worked it into the water. I remember that this concerned me deeply and I began to regard the holding back of the tears as a matter of secondary importance. Suddenly the raft was afloat and I felt it moving. I noticed with horror that it was receding from the shore and from my mother. My father, with the aid of the pole, was pushing it out from shore. This was too much. Casting an appealing look at my mother, I held out my arms toward her and broke down, blubbering out, "I shall never see my Mamma again."

This was too much for my soft-hearted mother. She, too, broke down and demanded that I be brought ashore at once. This was done amid derisive ridicule from my father. My mother and I retired to the house thoroughly discomfited. I was horribly disgraced and I was days recovering from the shame of having failed.

§ 3

One Sunday morning in Fanwood my father made the startling announcement that he was going to hypnotize a chicken. He had been reading about it in a scientific paper. I had not the remotest idea what hypnotize meant, and when I asked him what it meant he said, "You know—sort of mesmerize him." The trouble with this explanation was that I did not know what "mesmerize" meant. I was just as much at sea as ever. However, I knew it would be interesting, whatever it was, and I determined to be on hand.

He said that he would need some chalk and a chicken, and that, considering Mamma's way of regarding matters of this sort, we had better perform the

[41]

operation out in the barn. He asked me if I knew where we could find a piece of chalk. I remembered seeing a piece in a box containing some nails out in the barn, and we both went out to get it. The box was not where I expected to find it, but, looking around, I spied it on a beam. It was up too high for my father to look into, and he asked me why I thought there was any chalk in it. It seemed like second sight to him. I was positive about it and insisted that he get it down and look into it for a piece of chalk. He reached up, brought it down and, sure enough, there was the chalk in it just as I had said it would be. He was immensely amused and gave me that funny little look which I had grown to know meant that he thought I was bright. I used to treasure these little looks, for he was not easy to please.

Then we cleared away a place on the barn floor. I could see that the hypnotizing operation was going to require a lot of space. Then we went out to where the chickens were. He asked my opinion about which one we'd better hypnotize. He was very apt to ask my advice on matters of this sort, consulting me at length as though I were his equal. I have no doubt that I was very earnest and that he extracted a lot of fun out of my seriousness and the naïve answers of a child not yet six.

It was difficult to form any idea at all about which

chicken to pick out, because I had no notion as to whether it involved killing the chicken, or petting it, or feeding it, or what. After much mental fumbling around, he patiently awaiting my verdict, I told him that I did not know which chicken would be best because I did not know what he was going to do. Again he said, "Oh—you know—just mesmerize it."

This got us nowhere, and one of his favorite types of conversation then ensued.

"Well, what do you do to a chicken when you do that to him?" I asked, avoiding the word because I knew I should not be able to pronounce it.

"Do what to him?"

"That thing you said."

"What I said to the chicken?" This in a surprised tone.

"No, not that. That thing that you said you were going to do to the chicken. What do you do when you do it?"

"You mean, what does the chicken do?"

"No, not the chicken. You don't understand me, Papa." Getting up very close to him this time and doing everything in my power to impress the man, I said, "What do *you* do to the chicken?"

"Oh! You mean what do I do?"

"Yes—to the chicken."

"What chicken?"

"The chicken you were going to do that thing to."

"That's what I say. What chicken shall we do it to?"

"Now, Papa, you don't understand. I said, *'What-are-you-going-to-do-to-the-chicken?'* Can you understand that, Papa?"

"Oh yes, indeed! I can understand that all right. But what I am trying to find out is, do you think we better do it to a hen or a rooster."

This did not help any. I still did not know what it was he was contemplating doing, and until I knew, there was no way in which I could decide between a hen and a rooster.

"What is it you have to do?" I ventured once more.

"Who? Me or the chicken?"

"I said, *'What-is-it-you-have-to-do-to-the-chicken?'*"

"I don't *have* to do anything to the chicken. Do you?"

At about this stage of one of these cross purpose discussions I would be right up under his nose in my efforts to get him to understand, for not only was I an easy mark, but I was the personification of seriousness. Probably he would get where he no longer could contain himself, for he would break the combination by taking some entirely new slant. He selected a rooster without more ado and told me to chase him, to chase him slowly, not to catch him, but to keep running him until he told me to stop. This was nothing less than a gift from heaven, for I was strictly forbidden to chase the chickens and it was something I dearly loved to do. Here I was being sent to do it!

I selected the rooster which he had pointed out, and started to chase him. At first the rooster was very spry as well as thoroughly astonished. After a few minutes his wind gave out. I kept steadily after him, in and out and around, and it was as plain as anything could be that he was utterly at a loss to understand what in the world had suddenly happened. I clearly recall how he waddled from side to side as he became more and more tired and winded. When he began to show signs of becoming groggy and to droop his wings and waddle very badly indeed, my father called to me that that would be enough. He then caught the rooster, which in the latter's exhausted condition it was easy to do.

Carrying him into the barn, he sat him down on the barn floor, pushed his head down so that his beak was close to the floor, and placed the chalk directly in front of his beak. Moving the white chalk back and forth a bit to attract the bird's attention, my father held the creature motionless a moment and then slowly drew a broad white mark on the barn floor straight out from the rooster's beak. When the mark was about a foot and a half long he stopped. Then he arose, walked around, and waved his arms, as though to shoo the rooster away; but the creature never moved. He remained absolutely motionless, squatted down, staring at the chalk mark—completely mesmerized.

My father was delighted. He explained to me that the chicken was hypnotized or mesmerized and would remain in that condition for several minutes. He wanted to see how long the bird would remain mesmerized, so we sat down and watched it. I imagine we sat there something like three minutes, when the rooster seemed to awaken from a sleep. He raised his head, looked around, appeared to be surprised at his surroundings, gave a violent flap with his wings and ran out of the barn. Once out of the barn he hurried away, cackling indignantly.

§ 4

There came a time, probably in the fall of the year, when our pig must be slaughtered and dressed. It was a very important occasion and I recall that it was the cause of much discussion. We were city people and, except for my father, I suspect that we were a bit wanting when it came to farm technique. Looking back at it, I think the harrowing details of the slaughtering must have been kept from me. I seem to have no memory of anything connected with the passing of our pig until the poorer neighbors began coming around for parts of him. It must have been the custom to give to the poorer people those parts of a pig which a family such as ours would not be expected to need. I remember that there were people coming every day and that my soft-hearted mother gave them the feet, the head, the hide, the liver, and all the other things which a pig provides and which we were expected to give away.

One Sunday morning a very seedy and disreputable-looking man walked up to the front piazza on which my father and I were talking. After wishing each other good morning, the seedy one asked my father if he had given his soul to God. My father, not understanding him, and thinking that he was another applicant for a part of the pig, replied:

"I don't know. I'll ask my wife."

This seemed to surprise the seedy one, but my father arose, went into the house and, calling to my mother, who was upstairs, said, "Oh, Jane, there's a man down here asking for part of the pig!"

My mother, probably very busy with the baby, replied that we had given everything that we had to give and had no more. My father returned to the man and told him he was sorry, but that we had nothing more left to give away; what we had left we would like to keep for ourselves.

This appeared to surprise the seedy one more than ever. He did not seem able to comprehend, and the two men stared at each other, each wondering what was the matter with the other. I suspected trouble right away, for whenever a situation such as this arose with my father there was always trouble. Finally the man, mumbling in a very stupid fashion, repeated his original query. His delivery was very bad indeed and my father missed it again. Stepping down a step on the piazza stoop in order to be nearer, and turning his head to one side so that one ear would be pointed directly at the seedy one, he said, very energetically, "What's that?" This seemed to intimidate the seedy one. He became tongue tied for a moment during which the two men stared at each other in puzzlement. Finally the seedy one found his voice and repeated:

"Have you given your soul to God this beautiful Sabbath morning?"

My father got it right this time. Snapping his head around, he stared very hard at the seedy one a moment, then casting his glance around as though seeking some one from whom he might ask advice, he returned his gaze to the seedy one.

"You want to know if I have given my soul to God?" he repeated.

"Yes," answered the seedy one, waving his arms to take in the smiling landscape, and continuing, "On this beautiful Sabbath morning."

All this had offered time for my father to gather his wits. He proceeded in his characteristic manner. Turning abruptly to me, he said:

"Percy, this man wants to know if we have given our souls to God this beautiful Sabbath morning. Have you given yours?"

I had no very clear idea as to what was meant by a soul, but since I was positive that I had not given anything away since I got up that morning, I shook my head. I knew my father's methods and I was becoming concerned and very self-conscious.

Turning to the seedy one, he said, "My son here says he has not given his." Turning again to me, he asked, "Do you happen to remember whether your mother gave her soul to God this morning?"

This time I knew that I must speak, so I said, "I don't think she did, Papa."

Turning to the seedy one as though disappointed, he said, "I don't think any of us have, mister."

This literal point of view on the part of my father threw the seedy one into complete confusion. He was some sort of a poor miserable religious tramp looking for a dime or a quarter, probably dull witted to begin with, and utterly incapable of carrying on with my nimble-witted father. I imagine that he suggested to my father that he come up on the piazza and pray. My father thought this a good idea, so he asked him up and offered him a chair. There was some conversation which I do not remember, after which the seedy one started to get down on his knees.

"Hold on!" my father exclaimed. "Before you begin praying let's find out what the chances are that your prayers will be answered. Have you done much praying? Have you ever prayed before in your life?"

This shocked the seedy one. It was as plain as the nose on his miserable face that he spent most of his waking hours praying. Even I guessed that, had he spent a little less time praying and a little more time working, he would not look so miserable.

"Well, are your prayers any good? Do they work? Have they any pulling power?"

This knocked the seedy one speechless again for several moments. All he could do was to mumble.

"If your prayers will work, and if they will bring you anything you ask for, I am interested, because there are a lot of things I want," continued my father.

The seedy one was getting in deeper every minute. He

mumbled something about the beautiful Sabbath morning, the value of prayer, and a lot of other mixed-up stuff that had no meaning and which my father could not hear. I wondered how this thing was going to end.

Returning to his point, my father asked him if he had ever tried praying for a new suit of clothes. I thought this very much to the point indeed, for if there was one thing which the seedy one needed, it was a new suit of clothes. But he did not seem to have thought to pray for a new suit of clothes, which led my father to rebuke him. "Now see here, mister. If your praying never gets you anything, there must be something wrong with the way you pray. I've heard a lot lately about what prayers will do if they are the right kind. If I could find somebody who had some good, sure-fire prayers that would work I would like to get some of them. Now, I tell you what, there's no use praying just for the sake of praying. If you will get down on your knees and pray good and hard and loud, and will show results, I can get you a good job. I have a music-box in the parlor and it plays ten tunes if I wind it up tightly. Now, mister, if you will pray to have the music-box stopped, and it stops, then I shall know that you know how to pray and that your brand of prayers is a good brand. What do you say?"

The seedy one did not know what to say. He was not mentally competent to do much more than mumble a lot of meaningless words; but he could do this mumbling. Anyone could see that he had no idea of the proposition my father had made him. All he wanted to do was to get down on his knees and mumble, with the hope that ultimately he would get a dime or a quarter out of it. After a moment of painful silence my father arose, motioned the seedy one to follow, which he did like the poor miserable sheep that he was, and I joined in. My father led the way into the parlor, where he wound up our music-box, making quite sure that it really was wound up to the end. Then he started it playing. Turning to the seedy one, he said: "Now, mister, here's your chance. Get down on your knees and let me see you stop this music-box by prayer."

The seedy one did not know any better, or else he ached so to get going praying that he did not mind what else was involved; he got down on his knees, clasped his dirty hands under his chin, cast his bleary eyes to heaven, and in the most mournful voice I had ever heard, began praying. My father took up a position back of him, winked at me, and awaited results.

The music-box went on and on, pausing between tunes. These pauses would have encouraged me had I

been the seedy one. The praying went on and on, the
seedy one rolling his eyes in a positively ghastly manner
so that I did not like to look at him. I listened to what
he was mumbling, and as far as I could make out he
seemed to make no request to have the music-box
stopped. In fact, I could not seem to find anything that
he requested. I recall that it seemed to me that, had I
been doing the praying, I would have come out clearly
and flatly and asked to have the music-box stopped. But
this poor specimen of a man was short on ideas. He
used the same phrases over and over, appearing to de-
pend more upon a mournful tone of voice than upon
anything else. In the meantime the music-box raced
methodically on. Every time it came to the end of a
tune and paused, my heart stopped beating, wondering
if it were going to start the next tune. The strain was
terrible on me. When it finished the ninth tune there
seemed to be an especially long pause and I became
very tense indeed. I think my father was going through
the same experience, because he paid very close attention
during the pauses between tunes. But the music-box began the tenth and last tune and my father announced,
"This is the tenth and last tune."

At this critical moment the unexpected happened.
My mother walked into the room. A look of surprise
immediately spread over her face. Neither my father nor

I had expected this. The dear lady could make neither head nor tail of the picture which presented itself. What looked like a tramp was kneeling in the center of her parlor, hands clasped, rolling his eyes to heaven and praying soulfully; our music-box was galloping through a gay little tune; her husband was sitting in a chair, grinning from ear to ear; her son was sitting in another chair, probably staring his eyes out.

Turning to my father, my mother mouthed the words, "What's—he—doing?"

Such a situation could not be resisted by my father. Mouthing his answer in imitation of my mother, he replied, *"Praying."*

If anything was evident, it was certainly that the man was praying. This got my mother just exactly nowhere at all, which was what my father intended.

"Who—is—he?" mouthed my mother.

Shrugging his shoulders and holding upward the palms of both hands, he mouthed back, "I—don't—know."

My mother was not getting ahead. Poor lady, she was utterly stuck, unable to think of what to do next. She was fast becoming desperate, I could see.

"What's—he—praying—for?" she mouthed.

"To—stop—the—music-box," he mouthed back.

"To stop the music-box!" repeated my astonished

mother to herself, looking more puzzled than ever. Casting desperate glances around the room, she presented a picture of complete bewilderment which was excruciatingly funny to my father.

Tiptoeing nearer to him she mouthed, "Make—him —stop." To this my father frowned and purported to be shocked, indicating that anything such as stopping a man while he was praying was unthinkable. I could see that he conveyed the thought, "Stop a prayer! Oh my dear! Such things are simply not done!" Meanwhile the music-box was playing gaily along and the praying was proceeding. My mother was stumped. What to do under such circumstances she could not possibly imagine. While she was cudgeling her brains, trying to think of what steps to take, the music-box stopped. It had finished playing its ten tunes.

My father, quick to grasp that the seedy one must not be allowed to think that he had stopped the music-box, jumped to his feet; tapping the seedy one on the shoulder, he said: "That's all, mister. The music-box has finished its ten tunes. It did not stop."

The seedy one was for not stopping, either. He seemed to be having a good time listening to his own voice. My father went over to the music-box, shut down the lid, and indicated that the seance was over. Reluctantly, the seedy one arose. Anticipating any remarks he might make, which even I knew would be nothing but some mumbling and of no moment whatsoever, my father said to him:

"Now, Mister, I have given you a good chance, but you have failed. Your prayers are no good. They don't work. You go along now and hunt up some better prayers. Here's twenty-five cents to buy some dinner. You look as though you had not had a good one in a long time."

Taking him by the arm, he led him out to the piazza, started him down the steps, and wished him a good morning. As might be expected, the twenty-five cents overcame all objections and made the transaction quite satisfactory. Without a word and without a glance back, the seedy one walked down the path to the road and passed out of our lives forever.

My mother had followed the two men out onto the piazza. When the man had gone she turned to my father and asked, "What in the world have you been doing, Hiram?"

My father in a very judicial manner replied:

"Merely running a little test on the efficacy of prayer, my dear. This man claimed that he had some prayers which would work. To test him out I put him up against our music-box. He undertook to stop the music-box by prayer, but he failed miserably."

To this my mother ejaculated, *"Hiram!"* . . . "Who is he?" she asked, after a pause.

"I don't know. He just walked in off the road."

"What is his name?" continued my mother, no doubt wondering if he was a neighbor and whether my father had blasted our reputations.

"Judging by his appearance, I think his name must be 'The Seedy One.'"

Whenever this incident was referred to thereafter we invariably used the term, "The Seedy One."

§5

It must have been about this time, October, 1875, that a very important event happened to us in Fanwood. The doctor brought another little baby sister whose name was Addie. I was a bit over six and I remember very well the night the doctor brought her. We seemed to have a lot of people visiting us at the time. There was the doctor who was in and out every little while, a young lady who always dressed in white clothes, and one of my mother's friends. I never knew our house to be so full of people. My father did not go to business in New York for a few days and he did not seem to be very well. He seemed to be worried about something and was very quiet and subdued. My mother fell ill just at this time, which was particularly unfortunate, because she loved babies and she would have enjoyed this one so much if only she had not been taken sick just at this time.

The night the doctor brought the baby I thought the house was on fire. I got up out of bed when I heard all the running around downstairs, but I could not smell any smoke when I leaned over the banisters or at my open window, so I went back to bed, wondering what they could be doing, running around so much downstairs. The only thing I could think of was that our pet crows had done something particularly naughty. The next morning at breakfast I asked my father if the crows had done something naughty. He replied that he did not think so; at least he had not heard of anything. He asked me why I inquired. I told him that I had heard a lot of running around downstairs early in the night. For once in his life my father did not return with something in the way of a grotesque explanation. I noticed this and it disturbed me. It was as plain as could be that he did not feel well and I became convinced that he was coming down with something dreadful. So I said to him:

"I hope you are not going to have the same illness that Mamma has, Papa."

The lady in the white dress thought there was something funny about this; my father also thought it was funny, because he smiled a sickly smile and said he certainly hoped he was not. Just the same, he was far from being himself and I was very uneasy about him.

"I suppose that you and Mamma have eaten something that did not agree with you," I offered. This also impressed the lady in the white dress as being funny. My father acquiesced, but made no comment. This remark about eating something that did not agree had been made to me every time I had been upset, so I was glad of the opportunity to work it off on some one else.

Some time after this I was shown my new little sister. I remember my profound disappointment. I expected that this new sister would be much like little Florence, who was very pretty, had lovely curls, and a ribbon on the top of her head. But this new sister was very different indeed—in fact, painfully different. She was not at all pretty; she was homely according to my ideas; her complexion was very much too red; it was a sort of a dark red, which I considered less attractive than light red or pink; she seemed hopelessly stupid; she conveyed no hint that she knew me, although I was her brother; she could not talk; she had no teeth at all; she could not walk; and generally she seemed to me to be a good deal of a failure.

[59]

I gave much thought to the doctor's having brought the baby. I wondered where he got it. I asked my father about this. He told me that no doctor ever told where he got his babies, because everybody would be crowding in to get a baby, which would spoil everything; but he suggested that they grew on cabbages and that the doctor kept track of cabbages and always knew where to go and find a baby whenever one of his people wanted one. This was very interesting. We had cabbages, and I fell to wondering if it could have been possible that our doctor went to our cabbage patch for our baby. The more I thought of it the more likely it appeared. I made up my mind to go out and look over our cabbages. I might find another little baby sister that was an improvement on the one which the doctor brought; and it might be that I could find the cabbage from which the one we had had been picked.

I made a systematic examination of every cabbage in our garden. Not one of them had a baby on it nor anything that suggested that one might be growing; and I could find no cabbage that looked as though it had a baby picked from it recently. I made up my mind to ask my father to help me. But I found he had gone to his business in New York, so I was forced to give the matter up.

§ 6

It probably was in the summer of 1875 that my mother began taking me to Plainfield and allowing me to join her in having ice cream. Plainfield was two and one half miles from Fanwood. My mother drove over there frequently, probably to do her shopping and marketing, and probably made up her mind one day that I was old enough to be a companion and to be allowed to eat a plate of ice cream with her. I discovered at one of these little affairs that I had conversational abilities and that my mother and I could have a very good time together just conversing. I must have just emerged from the helpless child stage and entered the partially self-reliant boy stage. Being my father's son, and also her son, it was impossible that I did not possess something resembling a sense of humor. It became evident to me that there was a certain way to say a thing that made it irresistibly funny to my mother. And I must have had some of her nicely balanced sense of the fitting, for I struggled to avoid being "fresh," as so many of my young friends were.

These little ice-cream parties gave birth to a delightful comradeship that was to grow up between my mother and me. To reach the place where we had the ice cream we seem to have gone down some steps to a platform where there were tables and chairs and an awning. We sat at one of the tables and ice cream was brought. We could look out over a little pond while eating the ice cream and talking. Since then I have been to Monte Carlo, Nice, Bertolini's at Naples, Shepheard's at Cairo, and most of the other beauty spots where one sits and sips and looks out over the world; but the memory of none of them compares with the little ice-cream pavilion at Plainfield, New Jersey, where I used to go with my mother.

I suppose it was a very ordinary little place, with shabby tables, shabby awnings, shabby chairs, and a shabby little wooden building. I suppose the pond was a miserable little pond reeking with mosquitoes. But I saw it through the eyes of youth and inexperience, and it was transcendently beautiful.

The ice cream was the best in the world. Anyway, no ice cream in the world I have eaten since has compared with it. It had a flavor which no words could describe. I used to employ a system when eating it. I found that by scraping off the sides with my spoon that the ice cream would last longer and taste better. It was our practice to converse and eat very slowly. Our conversation had something about it which I never quite understood. Whether it was the brilliance of my wit, the sparkle of my conversation, or the way I ate the ice cream, I do not know to this day. However, one of them must have been very funny to my mother, for she always laughed a great deal on these occasions. No other recollections of mine are so sweet as those of the little ice-cream pavilion at Plainfield, New Jersey, and my mother.

§ 7

That I was rapidly becoming a man was borne in upon me when my father asked me to go with him to the Centennial Exhibition at Philadelphia. This invitation was extended to me one morning at breakfast. My father selected a moment when my mother was out of the room, as might be expected of him. Either I had learned not to hold back, or else I grasped upon any new idea naturally, for I recall that I pleased my father by accepting his invitation with enthusiasm. As far back as my memory went it had been his habit to take me with him to all sorts of places and, while there was a nervous strain connected with them, yet he was so interesting that the pleasant overbalanced the unpleasant.

I had no more idea what a centennial was than had my new baby sister. I imagine that I was told that it was the hundredth anniversary celebration of the signing of the Declaration of Independence; but all this passed off me as does water off a duck's back. My father was pleased at my enthusiasm, as I could tell by the funny little tell-tale lines around his eyes. From what I remember and from what has been told many times in my presence, I imagine the conversation ran something like this:

"You know what a Centennial is, of course."

I hesitated while I tried to remember; but I could not remember a solitary thing about centennials, so I answered, "Have I ever been to one?"

The funny little lines came back at this. I did not realize it, but it was considered a mighty good answer which put it up to him to find a suitable reply.

"Centennial exhibitions? Let's see. Why—you must have been to a lot of centennial exhibitions, Percy."

"Well—did I go to them with you, Papa?"

This is said to have driven him into a corner again; but I was too young to realize it.

"Seems to me we have. I cannot seem to remember," he said.

This emboldened me. If he could not remember he could not blame me for not remembering. By way of helping him, and recalling to his mind places I had been with him, I asked:

[64]

"Do they have cows or ice cream at them?" The cows were the Jersey City stockyards and the ice cream was the pavilion at Plainfield.

After a pause, which was probably necessary in order that he might control his voice, he said in a surprised tone, "Cows and ice cream, Percy?"

"Well, one place we went to they had a lot of cows and you gave them some water to drink. You remember that, don't you, Papa? And Mamma takes me to a place in Plainfield where they have ice cream. Are they cenlennials?" I knew that I did not have the word right when I saw the funny little lines come back.

"Oh yes. I remember. No, they are not cenlennials. They have cows and ice cream at cenlennials, but they have lots of other things, too—engines and locomotives. Big ones and small ones. They have a little locomotive and some cars which are too small for you to get into. You would have to sit on the roof of a car."

"I am sure I never went to a place like that, and I want to go and see that little train. Does it go by itself?"

"Yes, indeed. They build a fire under the boiler, get up steam and it goes choo-chooing along the little track just like a big train."

"Does it have a bell on it?"

"Yes, a bell and a whistle, just like a regular train.

[65]

It's exactly like a regular train—everything just the same, except that it's small."

I was bewildered. Of all the things I liked to look at, a steam locomotive held first place. Its noise hurt my ears and frightened me, but it was enthralling, nevertheless, as it is to every boy even to this day, the electric locomotive notwithstanding.

This conversation had gone on for some time when my mother returned. I caught my father's eye to ascertain his attitude toward telling my mother. A return nod indicated consent, so I launched into the Centennial matter. She cast a swift glance down to the other end of the table and appeared to be in doubt. This was disturbing because I wanted to go and see that little engine and train. The hitch in my mother's mind was that it would be my first overnight trip with my father. This meant nothing to me, but it was quite an occasion to them. I knew exactly how my father felt, because I remember distinctly when precisely the same circumstances arose in my own case, when I was a young father and I ventured forth for the first time for a few days with my young son.

My mother was not enthusiastic. She foresaw ill-advised jokes, tears on my part, ridicule on my father's part, and trouble generally. But she was won over and in due time the preparations for the great journey were made. She helped us off when the day came, kissed me good-by, and told me to be a good boy. With trembling lips and moist eyes she waved her hand as we drove away, and the greatest adventure in my life up to that time was on.

I can recall clearly our standing on the platform of the railroad station, waiting for the train to come, my hand in my father's, and I remember his explaining to acquaintances that he and his son were going to the Centennial at Philadelphia. I did not realize then, but I did when I grew older, that he was more impressed by my presence than I was by his.

The ride to Philadelphia is very hazy in my memory. I can remember my father disapproving the purchase of candy, an unheard-of proceeding on his part. My mother had to curb him every few minutes when she was along. But without her he was just as conservative on the candy business as she was. She would have marveled at him could she have known how he changed when she was not there. Instead of the heedless person, full of bluster and ridicule, who appeared to accept no responsibility, he was as watchful and solicitous as she was wont to be. All this is no more than should be expected of any father, but it was a very great deal more than was to be expected of my father.

We went hand in hand through the great Centennial Exhibition. To me it was like walking into a wonderful new world. I could not begin to take it in, but my father explained the things within my power of comprehension. We saw the little engine and train and I had several rides on it. We saw the big Corliss stationary steam-engine and I remember how it looked. But the thing we saw which stands out in my memory more distinctly than anything else, including the little engine and train, was something which never should have impressed a child at all. It was the 1,440-pound meteorite. I even remember its weight and the sign it had on it, for I was old enough then—nearly seven— to read a simple sign. When I stood before it and my father told me that it had fallen to our earth from the sky, that probably it had roamed around in the remote recesses of space for millions of centuries, and finally by accident had intercepted our earth, and that it was *not of our earth,* I felt a great wave of reverence and awe sweep over me. Such a profoundly impressive thought had never come to me before. I asked my father to take me back to the meteorite again and again, and I well recall how interested he was in my awe and wonderment. No doubt he knew precisely the feelings aroused in me, for it is more than likely that the same feelings were aroused in him.

The thoughts of that meteorite have remained with

me all my life. I have made pilgrimages to many other meteorites since, including those at the American Museum of Natural History in New York; and today, as I stand before them, I never fail to think of that first one at the Centennial in Philadelphia before which I stood as a small child, my hand in my father's and my mind hungering to know more about such things.

I imagine that my father and I spent several days at the Centennial. I remember that I slept in the same bed with him, which was very exciting, and I remember the interesting matters of which we talked before we went to sleep. I do not recall one unpleasant or painful moment during this entire trip, and I suspect he enjoyed it just as keenly as I did.

PART III

WE MOVED back to Brooklyn late in 1877 after purchasing a house on Union Street. I was considerably more of a boy by this time, being able to hold my own with other children and being also less dependent upon my mother. After we became settled my father resumed taking me with him on various expeditions on Sunday.

I have a very vivid memory of one of these. My father wanted to find one of his former machinists whose name was Baskerville. I believe he wanted to induce him to return to work. He did not know Baskerville's address, some time having elapsed since he last had heard from him, but selected the most likely address and we investigated it one Sunday morning. The neighborhood was very unprepossessing, the houses being wooden, in bad repair and very shabby generally. The number we sought turned out to be a house with a high wooden stoop in a shocking state of disrepair. We walked up this dreadful stoop and my father pulled the bell handle at the shabby front door. There were no push buttons and no electric bells in those days.

I heard the bell jangle in the recesses of the house. There was a long wait during which my father and I stood in silence and surveyed the depressing aspect of the street. Then I heard footsteps within the house. They grew louder and louder, indicating the approach of some one from a considerable distance. Then I heard a bolt drawn, a chain unhooked, and a lock thrown, after which the door was opened about four inches, disclosing a black interior and a peculiarly repellent hatchet-faced woman in most slattern attire. I think this woman looked so perfectly awful that she non-plused my father for an instant; but he found his voice and said, in his most ingratiating manner, "Good morning. Can you tell me if Mr. William Baskerville lives here?"

This was done in a very gentlemanly manner, and by no stretch of the imagination calculated to give offense. But the hatchet-faced woman snapped back, "No! He don't!" and slammed the door in my father's face. I could hear the lock turned, the chain hooked, and the bolt sliding into place, and then the footsteps receding. My father gazed at me in amazement. I became concerned, for my father was not a person with whom to take such liberties. However, he turned, slowly descended the steps, and started back home. Not a word was spoken. I followed like a little dog, watching him closely, for I found it difficult to believe that he was beaten. He went on, head bent in thought and obviously deeply chagrined. I wondered if it possibly could be that he at length had met his match. Was he going to accept such an insult? It was unthinkable. Nevertheless, here he was, slinking away like a whipped dog.

As I wondered, he suddenly turned and started back. That settled it! I had misjudged him. He was the same old chap. He was going back and he was going to make trouble. I had to follow, but it was with a heavy heart, for I knew him and I knew that there would shortly be an unpleasant scene. If only my mother were here to reason with him; she could always control him. But she was not present and there was no escape. I must see the unpleasant business through. Thus in silence we walked back to the house.

Arriving at the rickety stoop, we walked straight up as though we had never been there before. He pulled the door-bell handle exactly as before. I could hear the dreadful thing jangle in the recesses of the house exactly as before. Again came the long wait, during which we stood in silence and viewed the unprepossessing prospect. Again the approaching footsteps. They came to the door exactly as they had before. I heard the same bolt drawn, the same chain unhooked, and the same lock turned. Finally the door opened as before. There

stood the same hatchet-faced slattern. When she saw
the same man and little boy standing there she seemed
completely surprised. My father, in the same well-modu-
l_ted tones as before, repeated exactly what he had said
before: "Good morning. Can you tell me if Mr. Baskerville lives here?"

For a moment the woman paused. She did not know
what to make of the situation. Then in tones even more
acid and emphatic than she had used before she snapped
out, "*No!! He don't!!!*" As quick as the wink of an eye
and before she had time to slam the door, my father
snapped back at her, imitating her tone and voice as
closely as he could, "*Well, who the hell said he did?*"
Then we went back home.

§ 2

A time came when my mother grew concerned over
my father's health. He had led a very active country
life during his youth, and our city life with its days
and nights of unremitting toil, with no exercise in the
open air, were beginning to tell upon even his rugged
physique. He was among those who organized the
United States Electric Lighting Company, one of the
pioneers in the electric-lighting field. He was chief engineer and he was struggling with might and main to

develop an arc and an incandescent lighting system. He spent his days in New York and he spent half of his nights over a drafting-table at home, working until very late and allowing himself but a few hours of sleep. He worked just as he played. It was a feverish, desperate rush or it was nothing at all.

My mother urged him to take an hour every evening and exercise in the open air. She finally had her way, as she always did, for he was the essence of amenability with her. And so it came about that one evening about seven-thirty he asked me to come along with him and take some exercise. I might have known that the exercise which he would take would be characteristic of him and unlike anything ever heard of before.

It should be remembered that business men in New York in the time of which I write wore high silk hats and Prince Albert coats. We walked up to Court Street, which was a business street having a horse-car line. At seven-thirty in the evening Court Street's sidewalks were always well filled. Arrived here, my father said to me: "Come along, Percy. Let's get some exercise." With this, he reached up and pulled his silk hat down upon his head, bringing it to his ears and pushing it entirely too far back on his head. He buttoned up his Prince Albert coat and, stepping out into the middle of the

[74]

street, started running toward City Hall with all his might.

There was nothing for me to do but to follow. But I winced at the spectacle we were making of ourselves. I wondered what my friends would think; I wondered what the people on the sidewalks would think; and what was more to the point, I wondered what the police would think, seeing a man in a silk hat, which was jammed down to his ears and very much too far back on his head, running madly down the middle of the street, followed by a small boy. The whole affair impressed me as being in extremely bad taste; but there was nothing I could do about it. He would have been very difficult had I failed to join him in the running.

I had all I could do to keep up with him. As a matter of fact, I was compelled to get right down to business and run just about as fast as I could. But I saw that he made much heavier weather of it than I did. He had a lot more weight to carry and the cobblestones were rough for him. I knew that the going was much easier near the horse-car rails. I was astonished at the tremendous power he was exerting. It seemed to me there was danger of his tearing up the paving-stones, putting all that power into propelling himself. He had headed east toward City Hall, as we called Borough Hall in those days. We passed Sackett Street going like the wind. At Degraw Street the speed had slackened off perceptibly. Somewhere about Butler Street he became completely winded and stopped, looking back in the distance for me. But I was immediately behind him, which seemed to cause him surprise. He no doubt thought, from the exertion which he was making, that he had left me away behind. He did not realize that I spent a large share of my time running on those streets.

He limped over to the sidewalk. Here he sought out a post against which he leaned heavily. He puffed like nothing human. I never saw a person so utterly spent. I waited in silence for the next move, much like a well-trained dog. I was breathing deeply, but I was far from being completely exhausted as he was.

He tried to say something, but he could not articulate. In a few minutes he partially recovered, straightened his hat, for which I was very glad, and wheezed something to the effect that we better walk home slowly. I was very glad to do this, because I really feared that the police would be after us. It seemed to me remarkable that we had not aroused the entire street, setting everybody to running; for if ever I saw anything that looked like a convincing escape, it was my father tearing with all his might down the middle of Court Street.

He limped badly as we walked slowly home. When I asked him why he had gone lame he said that the cobblestones had hurt his feet. By the time we reached home he was very lame. In addition, he looked as though he were very ill indeed. My mother was calmly reading in the reception-room when we walked in. He went directly to her and, drawing up a chair very close to hers, he wilted into it. She calmly and deliberately put down her book and started to ask him if he had had a nice walk, when she caught sight of his face, his general state of collapse, and his unexpected proximity. Startled, she exclaimed, "Why, Hiram! What's the matter?"

He had a queer way with him when he did not feel well. It was to gaze steadily and very gloomily into my mother's face at very close range, giving the impression that he awaited her assistance, or was about to burst into tears, or die. He would say nothing at these times. He always reminded me of a big dog when he did this. He had large brown eyes, and as he sat gazing pleadingly into her face, with his own not six inches away and with an expression which suggested nothing less than that the bottom had dropped out of everything and that his last friend had deserted him, he certainly resembled a big and a very mournful Newfoundland dog. My poor mother never failed to fall for this sort of thing. It was obvious that most of it was put on and yet she never seemed to realize this. Sometimes I thought that I knew him better than she did. She took him literally, the one thing which should not be done with him.

Deeply concerned, my excitable little mother jerked herself around and repeated, "Hiram! What's the matter with you?"

Offering absolutely no response at all, he continued to gaze sadly and pleadingly into her eyes at very close range. My mother always wore spectacles. Readjusting these and lifting her face slightly so as the better to look through them, she peered at him intently. For the moment that the two of them sat there gazing at each other in silence, their faces not more than a few inches apart, I thought I had never seen anything funnier.

Jumping to her feet, she put her arm around him, stroked his head, and in a frightened voice asked me to tell her exactly what had happened. I waited a moment for him to do the explaining, but as he gave no indication of doing it, I told her that we had run down Court Street and Papa had hurt his feet on the cobblestones. At this my mother stopped stroking his head and directed her attention to his feet. He lifted one leg limply and held out his foot to her, wheezing, hoarsely, "Please take it off, Jane."

Men wore what were called "congress gaiters" in

those days. They had elastic sides and they could be pulled off. She pulled the shoe off the foot offered her, and then with a show of the greatest difficulty, and as though his strength were fast ebbing, he held out the other foot. She pulled the shoe off and examined his feet. There seemed nothing wrong and, looking critically at his face again, she said, "Hiram, tell me what has happened."

He replied in a wheezy whisper, "You nearly killed me, Jane."

"*I* nearly killed you, Hiram! For mercy's sake, what did I do?"

After great effort and much grotesque gulping, which suggested a person in the last throes of something very dreadful, he managed to get out, "*Exercise.*" I caught on right here. He was going to try and blame my mother because he felt badly after exercising.

"Did the exercise hurt your feet?" All she got from this was an affirmative and a very sickly nod.

"Does it hurt you to walk?"

His reply to this was to hold up both his hands, roll his eyes to heaven, and then point to his stockinged feet, which he then managed to curl up and make appear frightfully deformed. This very nearly sickened my sensitive mother. She recoiled at those two "deformed" feet, not daring to look at them again. She took another long and close look at his face, which did look quite haggard, for the man had grossly fagged himself. Convinced that she had a sick husband on her hands, she arose and in her decisive little way announced, "You must go right to bed this minute and I shall send for the doctor. Come along." She began assisting him to his feet.

He laboriously arose, like a very aged man who was perilously close to collapse, and we thought he was going upstairs and to bed; but, instead, he laid himself down on the sofa. I began to feel concerned myself at this turn of affairs, and I wondered if he really were ill. He dispelled this notion in the next moment. Regaining his normal voice entirely, he said, quite briskly, "Jane, you nearly killed me. It was you who made me go out and exercise. It nearly killed me."

"Nearly killed you, Hiram! What do you mean?"

"You made me go out and exercise, didn't you?"

"I didn't *make* you go, Hiram. I thought it would do you good."

"Well, it nearly killed me, Jane."

"For mercy's sake, what sort of exercise did you take?"

"I ran with all my might nearly down to City Hall with Percy for exercise. I simply could not run any farther."

"Ran down nearly to City Hall! What do you mean
—*ran?"*

"Just ran. Did you never see anybody run, Jane?"

"Do you mean to tell me that you *ran* down Court
Street to City Hall, Hiram?"

"We did just what you told us to do. Didn't we,
Percy? You told us we needed exercise, and we went
out and got a lot of it in a few minutes. I did my best
to get to City Hall for you, Jane, but my strength gave
out. I don't think you realized how far it is to City
Hall when you made me go out and run there. I must
be getting old and feeble." Whereupon he heaved a
deep sigh.

The conversation went on in this strain for quite a
while, my father taking the position that he had gone
to the very limits of his strength, even to flirting with
death, in his efforts to obey my mother's instructions
to go out and get some exercise. She tried to explain
that she never expected him to run with all his might
until he dropped from utter exhaustion. And besides,
what would people think, seeing a man of his position
running with all his might down the middle of Court
Street?

After half an hour of blaming her for nearly causing his death, he pulled on his shoes with vigor, gave her
one of his bear hugs, kissed her into partial suffocation,

and went to work on his drafting-board. Poor lady! She lived an eventful life, what between her temperamental husband and her three temperamental children.

§3

In the development of the incandescent electric lamp, one of the difficulties the pioneers experienced was the pumping of a satisfactory vacuum in the glass bulb. Mercury, or as it used to be called, quicksilver, was used in the process. My father brought home a small bottle half filled with it. I do not know, but I suspect that his sole object in bringing it home was to have some fun with the family.

Our Union Street house was what was known as an English basement arrangement. There was a brown-stone stoop of some five steps which led to a vestibule and thence to the front door. This gave into the main floor of the house. This main floor had a long hall, a reception- or living-room, a dining-room and a butler's pantry. The kitchen was immediately below the dining-room. A "dumb waiter," or small hand-operated elevator, brought things up from the kitchen to the butler's pantry, whence they were served to the dining-room. The butler's pantry was a long room with a sink, a long row of cupboards, and a clothes-closet in which were kept overcoats, rubbers, umbrellas, and canes. It was in this closet that we children were made to shut ourselves when we were naughty. The cupboards in the butler's pantry contained many things besides the dining-room tableware, and so it was natural that my father should be fussing at the cupboards when the little family filed into the dining-room one Sunday.

As we were taking our seats my father burst into the dining-room from the butler's pantry. He had hold of something which seemed to be terribly hot. He pranced around, shifting the hot object from one hand to the other, snatched a napkin off the table, hissed with the pain, and was desperately endeavoring to avert being badly burned, when my startled mother rushed to him, holding out her skirts and saying: "Here, Hiram. Drop it here."

My father did not seem to understand that she was holding out her skirts to receive the hot object. He had his back to her, and when she ran around to get in front of him he stupidly turned the other way, so that she was still back of him. Seeing that my father's hands were being burned in consequence, I shouted at the top of my lungs, "Papa, Papa, look! Give it to Mamma!" But he could not seem to be made to understand that she was there with her skirts held out.

"Here, Hiram. Here. Drop it here, Hiram!" she kept urging, doing everything in her power to get in front of him; but every way she turned he turned the opposite way, prancing and hissing and giving the impression that he was in terrible pain. I added my shouts, being very much excited, while little Florence looked on in frightened amazement and did her best to keep from being underfoot. Seeing that something ought to be done right away, I started around the table to lay hold of my father and twist him around by brute force so he could see my mother with her skirts held out. He hissed something about melted lead in a bottle and I caught sight of a metallic-looking liquid in a bottle. Little Florence kept getting underfoot and the maid got snarled up in it; everybody was bumping into everybody else in utter confusion, and it was apparent that unless something were done, and done quickly, my father's hands would be horribly burned. As I was smaller and more agile than any of the grown-ups, I jumped into the fray, fought my way to the center of things, and snatched the bottle of "melted lead" out of my father's hands and snapped it into my mother's outstretched skirts. My father was taken aback. It had not occurred to him that I could act quickly enough to snatch the bottle away from him. To my amazement, the bottle was cool to the touch. I expected to feel the sting of the heat, but I thought that if I were quick enough I would not be burned.

Quiet fell as suddenly as the noise and confusion had arisen. For a moment all of us stood transfixed, staring at the bottle in my mother's skirts. My father looked very sheepish, which led me to suspect a joke somewhere. I came out of my trance first, and reached forward to snap my fingers across the bottle to test its heat. My father shouted: "Look out! It's hot!" But I had felt no heat when I snatched it from him, so I persisted, and again brushed quickly across it with my hand. There was no sensation of heat at all, so I made to pick it up. Both mother and father shouted at me to look out; nevertheless, I insisted, and put my hand directly on it. It was perfectly cool! I picked it up, which threw my mother into a panic, causing her to urge me to put it down. But I did not have to put it down; so I held it up to her, saying: "It isn't hot at all, Mamma. Feel of it."

The jig was up and my father walked away and sat down at his place at the table and indicated that he was ready for his dinner. I induced my mother to hold the bottle in her hand, which she did, casting an exasperated look at my father. She then delivered herself of her standard exclamation, "Hiram!" and sat down. In the meantime, I had acquired the bottle of mercury.

[85]

My father let me keep it. I had never heard of such a material. Its weight fascinated me; and it certainly did look like melted lead.

§ 4

We had a peach tree in our back yard at Union Street. I had noticed that something grew on the tree, but it was such a miserable-looking, dried-up sort of thing that I could not imagine what it might be. One day I took one of the miserable specimens to my father and asked him what it was. He asked me where I had obtained it, for it was such a very wretched thing that even he was in doubt about it. I told him that I got it off our peach tree in our back yard.

"Oh!" said he. "That's a peach."

"A peach!" I exclaimed, in wonder. "I never saw a peach that looked like that."

"Well, it's not much of a peach, Percy; but, you see, our tree never has any fertilizer put on it, and it's an awfully old tree, and in consequence it is starved. When a tree is starved, it can't grow good peaches."

I thought about this very seriously. It seemed a pity to have a peach tree and not get any peaches off it, because peaches were good and it would be very wonderful if we could grow our own peaches right in our own back yard. So I said to him:

"Papa, how could we fix our tree so it would have nice peaches on it?"

Whatever led the man to answer as he did is more than I shall attempt to explain. He said:

"Oh, I don't know exactly what we could do to it. I suppose the best thing to do is to get an old dead cat and bury it at the foot of the tree."

"An old dead cat!" I repeated in astonishment. "Would an old dead cat make peaches grow on our peach tree?"

"Oh yes, indeed! Grow like anything. If you got an old dead cat and buried it at the foot of the tree, good peaches would grow all right."

"Well, how long would it take for them to grow?"

"How long would it take before you got good peaches?" he asked.

"Yes. How long?"

I suspect that he began to formulate a scheme at this point. Up to this time he had merely been idly answering my questions.

"Well, Percy, I should say that if you buried a good big cat under the tree today, you probably would have plenty of beautiful peaches about tomorrow morning."

This sounded too good to be true. I expected him to say a year, and a year was a very long time to have to wait. If a fine crop of peaches could be grown from one day to another, I proposed to find an old dead cat and bury it under the tree. At the time of which I write, dead cats were frequently seen on the streets. I had seen many of them. There was no highly organized street-cleaning department in those far-off days, as there is now, and such a minor detail as a dead cat was left around until it disappeared naturally. I have no idea what became of all the dead cats I had seen in the streets.

For the next few days I was on the lookout for a dead cat. I inquired among my friends, but none of them could recall seeing a dead cat recently. I finally persuaded one of my friends to join me in a dead-cat hunt. We knew many vacant lots and we decided to visit them. After searching several we found in one of them the carcass of a cat. It must have been dead a very long time for it was very dry and very flat. But I hurried home with it.

Something told me that my mother would never approve of my bringing a dead cat into the house; so I decided to take it in through the basement and so on out into the back yard, where I could hide it easily. I did this and then awaited my father's return from business.

When he returned he brought another man with him, which was disconcerting. It broke up my plan for burying the cat. It must have been a Saturday when he brought this friend home, because the next day was Sunday. There was no way for me to bring up the dead-cat matter that evening, so I decided to see my father about it as early as possible Sunday morning.

Immediately after breakfast on Sunday morning he and his friend went out on the back stoop and sat down to talk. I had to get at my father somehow, and after much deliberation, I decided to go up and whisper in his ear that I had the dead cat. Once he knew that I had it, I was sure that he would find a way to put through the job of burying it. Without more delay, and as he was talking to his friend, I went up to him, put my mouth to his ear, and whispered, "Papa, I've got the dead cat." He stopped his talking and shot me a surprised look, for probably the matter had not entered his head since the original discussion.

"You've got what, Percy!" he exclaimed out loud.

Putting my mouth to his ear again, I said, "The dead cat!"

"*Dead cat*, Percy!" he exclaimed, again out loud and thoroughly surprised.

"Sh-h-h-h!" I warned. "Mamma will hear. You remember, Papa, don't you—the peaches."

"O Lord! Why, of course—the peaches!" he replied. Then in a low voice and adopting my furtive manner, he whispered, "Where is it?"

[89]

"Down by the grape arbor under a box," I whispered back.

I had interrupted his conversation when I first whispered to him; but this seemed to be acceptable. He evidently considered the dead-cat matter as of more importance than what they had been discussing. In a low tone he told his friend that he and his son had been figuring on a method to get peaches to grow on our tree, and that a dead cat was needed because, as every one knew, if a dead cat is buried at the foot of a peach tree it brings peaches right out. The friend acquiesced and indicated that it was a well-known phenomenon.

Turning to me, my father asked, "Where did you get the dead cat, Percy?" I told him that another boy and I had made a search of all the vacant lots and we had found one and brought it home. He seemed quite interested in this phase of the matter, even to asking me how I got it in without Mamma knowing about it. I told him that I had brought it in through the basement.

"How did you carry it?" he asked.

"By the tail," I replied.

"Did you drag that cat through the streets by the tail?" he inquired, smiling. I told him that I had, wondering why he should be interested in such a detail. He slapped his leg and laughed heartily. Then he went on:

"Well now, Percy, I tell you what. You go and fetch the coal shovel and we will bury it right away. Then we shall wait and watch the peaches come out."

This was very fine. Things were working splendidly. I fetched the coal shovel from the coal-hole and the three of us went out to the peach tree. My father started digging the hole and I went after the dead cat. It was but a few minutes' work for him to dig a deep enough hole, after which we pushed the dead cat in and started covering it up. We were almost finished when my mother called out from the window of her room, asking what we were doing. This disconcerted me, for I feared she might not approve burying dead cats under the peach tree; but my father replied that we were fertilizing the peach tree so that better peaches would grow. This satisfied her, although she said afterward that it seemed very strange that Papa should take such an interest in the peach tree all of a sudden.

When the job was finished I asked my father how long it would be before the peaches would grow. Looking at his watch, and casting a meaning look at his friend, he answered:

"Oh, sometime this afternoon. They ought to be pretty good by late afternoon, I should say."

It seemed wonderful to me that a dead cat should so enliven a peach tree that there would be a crop of peaches by late afternoon; but my father had said so and he knew.

I imagine that my sister Florence and I went to Sunday school about this time. In any event, we were absent for a couple of hours. We returned just before dinner at one o'clock. During this interval my father and his friend must have gone out to a fruit store and purchased a basket of very large peaches. They must have brought them home and my father must have climbed the peach tree and stuck the peaches on the twigs of the tree. It certainly must have been quite a labor. All this was entirely unknown to me.

Just before one o'clock little Florence and I came home. I had forgotten about the peach tree. My father and his friend were still out on the back stoop, talking. My mother came down for dinner, stepped out to join them, and I could hear her exclaiming over something my father had done; but as this exclaiming on her part occurred every hour in the day, I paid no attention to it.

Presently my father shouted, "Percy! Percy! Come quickly!" I dropped what I had and dashed out to the back stoop, knowing that something big had happened.

"Look!" he exclaimed. "The peaches are out!"

One look and I was staggered by the sight. The tree was loaded with peaches!

I made a rush for the tree and was up in it in a moment. Shouting to my mother to hurry and bring a basket, I began picking the peaches. I remember to this day my intense excitement and also my surprise at finding that the peaches were impaled upon the little twigs. I had not expected to find that they grew that way. I picked the peaches off, shouting in excited tones to those below to catch them in something soft so they would not be injured, and calling my mother's attention to the enormous size of the peaches and the number of them. It seemed to me I had never participated in anything so exciting in all my life. Presently they were all picked and I came down out of the tree. I was amazed. There was a basket full of peaches. I did not know that they had been taken out of the same basket within the hour. The most astonishing thing in the whole matter to me was the potency of the dead-cat treatment. It was several years before I caught on to this peach joke. For a long time I thoroughly believed that the planting of the dead cat had produced the peaches.

§ 5

There was a gas street lamp in front of our house on Union Street. As we sat on the front stoop on summer evenings I noticed that a bird would frequently fly close to this street lamp. I fell to wondering what sort of a bird flew around at night. When the opportunity arose I asked my father about it. I suppose I asked in a manner that interested or amused him, for he dwelt at length on the general subject of bats. He knew how to talk in a most interesting manner and he never failed to fascinate me when I succeeded in getting him going. I had never heard of a bat. I had supposed that anything which flapped its wings and flew must be a bird. That there should be a little flying animal, with fur on him just like a mouse, and teeth instead of a beak, that could fly and pick bugs out of the air on the wing at night impressed me profoundly. I suppose I pestered him with questions about bats all evening.

From that time on I wanted to catch a bat and have a look at him. That he was an animal and not a bird fascinated me. I recall how I used to steer the conversation to the subject of bats whenever the opportunity arose. Like a boy with a brand-new and absorbing idea, I wanted to talk about it all the time. So often did I say that I wished that I might catch a bat sometime, it is not to be wondered that my father turned his attention to the matter.

One Sunday morning while I was playing in our back yard I heard my father shout, "Percy! Percy! Come quickly!"

This was always an emergency call and it had an

electric effect upon me. Experience had shown that it meant something very important indeed. I must have been a very impetuous little boy, for I remember that I was always going everywhere at full speed. The instant I heard my father's voice calling I always dropped everything where it happened to be and ran with all my might. Stairs were taken two or three at a jump, doors were all but jerked off their hinges and left to close themselves. When I arrived at my destination I invariably was traveling too fast, and either had to stop by bumping into somebody or something, or by catching hold of some convenient object.

My father was in the butler's pantry. I skidded on all the turns in the dining-room and when I arrived where my father was standing beside the opening to the dumb-waiter well I crashed into him and came very near upsetting him. I took him completely by surprise.

"What is it?" I gasped.

"There's a bat down the dumb-waiter well," he whispered, pointing down the dark well. The dumb-waiter was at the bottom at the time. I peered down into the dark well, and sure enough, there was a black object fluttering back and forth down near the bottom.

"Gosh, Papa! Let's catch him." I was now more excited than ever. I remember the occasion as though it were but yesterday. I believed that haste was of paramount importance, because as long as he was down the dumb-waiter well we could get at him and the advantage would be ours; but the moment he got out the advantage would be his. Haste was absolutely essential. I said to my father, "Don't let him up, Papa!" while I bustled around the butler's pantry searching for something with which I could reach down and whack the bat. My father was a serious handicap. He was in my way every turn I made. I suppose the poor man could not help it, because the butler's pantry was narrow and I was darting around like a fly. I bumped into him every second.

The only thing I could find in the few desperate seconds I dared take to search was an umbrella. I grabbed it in the clothes-closet. It was hopelessly short, as I knew it would be. I tried it, doing my level best, reaching down as far as I could stretch. I had my father hold my legs so that I could be let down into the well as far as possible, but it was no use. The umbrella was too short. Up to this point I had not landed one single blow. I knew that unless I disabled the bat immediately he surely would fly out of the well and then I should lose him.

I wriggled myself back and, looking at my father, probably with wild eyes and a very red face because of hanging head down, I exclaimed:

"It's too short! What can we get that's longer?" But his mind was entirely too slow-acting. Besides, he was laughing so much that the tears were running down his face, a matter to which I attached no significance, strange as it appears now. It was plain that if I left the matter to him the bat surely would get away. My mind was working like lightning. Before I finished speaking I had an idea.

"A broom!" I exclaimed; and while he was getting the idea through his head I was off to the kitchen like a mad thing, shouting as I went, "Don't let him up, Papa!"

The brooms were in the basement. I dashed out of the butler's pantry, through the dining-room, into the hall, ricocheting off the walls in order to make the turns, plunged down the basement stairs two steps at a lick, grabbed and twisted the door knob at the foot of the stairs and releasing the door just as my body struck it —I was thoroughly practiced in this delicate maneuver —rushed for the brooms, grabbed the first one my hand fell upon, and tore back upstairs. Of course, all of this made a lot of noise which was heard all over the house, causing my mother, who was on the second floor, to wonder what could be going on.

With the broom in my hand I made a dive for the dumb-waiter well. By rare good luck, it seemed to me,

the bat was still there. The broom worked just as I believed it would. It was long enough to reach and it was
broad enough so I did not often miss. I landed my first
blow fairly and squarely. To my surprise, it did not
disable the creature. I whacked and whacked at the
thing until my arms ached. I was hanging head down
in a perfect smother of dust. The creature had the most
amazing vitality. I hit him fairly several times. One
trouble which I recognized was that the dumb-waiter
well was too small to allow me a satisfactory back
stroke. I could hit the bat, but there was not enough
power in the blow. I tried to add as much push as I
could after I landed on him; but he seemed to survive
the most savage attacks I could make. And thus the
battle raged, I whacking with all my might, kicking up
a most terrible dust, and, what with the whacking and
kicking with my shoes against the wooden wall of the
dumb-waiter shaft and my shouts to my father, making
a fearful noise. All this time my father was at the top
of the well, hanging on to my legs—and in spasms. I
had never seen the man laugh so. His eyes streamed
water. Curiously enough, this seemed of no significance
to me. He often laughed at my impetuous way of doing
things.

The reason that I could not disable the "bat" was
because it was made from a black bow which my father

had snipped off of one of my mother's hats. This black bow had been attached to a stiff wire which was fastened to the top of the dumb-waiter well. The springy wire caused the bow to flutter back and forth. In the semi-dark it could be mistaken very easily for something alive.

I fought that "bat" for a long time. I became so tired that I was groggy; but I dared not leave my commanding position at the dumb-waiter outlet for fear the thing would fly out and escape.

The awful noise caused my mother to investigate. When she came into the butler's pantry the picture which presented itself to her was nothing short of astounding. All she could see of me were my legs, clutched in my father's hands, he being in stitches of laughter. His head was held to one side as far as he could get it in an attempt to get a breath of fresh air. The dust was extraordinary. I heard my mother saying something, but I was far too busy to give attention to it. Finally she insisted on my coming up out of the well. I shall never forget my father's expression as we looked at each other when I came up. His eyes were streaming and he could hardly stand up. I was nearly exhausted and probably very dirty-faced, wild-eyed, and as full of fight as a terrier at a rat. I do not blame my father for being completely overcome.

"Look out, Papa! Don't let him up!" I shouted at the very top of my lungs as soon as I could speak.

My mother tried to calm me down, saying it was not a real bat at all and that I must come away and sit down and be quiet. But all that was utterly out of the question. I stood at her knee and she had both hands on my arms, talking to me very seriously. But she did not understand. Here was a bat. He was cornered. We must get him at all hazards. Such an opportunity would never come again. Still in a state of suppressed excitement, I called to my father:

"Here, Papa. You try it. Take the broom." But he was not inclined to get into the game. "Don't let him up, Papa," I kept urging.

My mother continued reasoning with me, insisting that I control myself, speaking very calmly and seriously and wiping my sweaty and dirty face. But not until I saw my father reach in, unfasten the wire, and pull up the "bat," did I understand the hoax. What hurt me was the disappointment that I was not to catch a real bat.

When the "bat" was retrieved my mother recognized it immediately. Rushing to the clothes-closet, she returned with her hat. Thrusting it in my father's face she demanded to know what he meant by daring to cut a bow off her best hat. His defense was that no one would know whether a bow had been taken from the hat or not; that a woman's hat was such an indeterminate object that such a detail as one bow more or less was of no moment. I would think twice before I undertook to snip a bow off my wife's hat, and I think most men would; but my father would not hesitate a moment. If the bow exactly fitted a need it would be snipped, whether it was on a hat or anything else.

§ 6

As I grew older it was natural that I should become more and more of a problem to my mother. My besetting sins were teasing my sisters and breaking things around the house. Finally a day came when I did a thing which my mother felt was beyond her.

She had a full-length pier glass in her room which extended from the floor to the ceiling. It had a white marble base with a flat place on the latter which extended out into the room about a foot. Little Florence discovered that a large glass marble would bounce beautifully off this base. One day she was bouncing her marble in front of the pier glass, and it occurred to me that it would surprise her very much were I to snatch the marble while it was in the air. I edged up, and when I was within reach I make a quick pass to snatch the marble. But I miscalculated. Instead of closing my hand upon it, I struck it with my hand and knocked it against the pier glass, which it broke.

I told my mother, and when she came upstairs and beheld her broken mirror she sank into a chair and wept. I was desolated. It hurt me inexpressibly that I should be the cause of my mother's weeping. She told me that I had got beyond her control and that she would have to turn me over to my father for a good whipping; that I paid no attention to her, and as things were going there was no living with me.

Turning me over to my father for a good whipping was a brand-new idea to me. I could not remember that my father had ever laid a hand upon me, except possibly once when I was very young indeed, when he tapped me gently with the tongue of his draftsman's T-square. This was very light and very thin and stung for a moment. It would not bruise. It is an admirable instrument for administering a little corporal punishment.

That evening after my father had come home he was led up to the broken pier glass and shown my latest and worst offense. It appeared to prostrate him utterly. He sank into a chair, held his head in his hands, rocked back and forth in exquisite agony, and gave several similar indications of being completely undone by the spectacle. He made it an extremely painful scene for me and I certainly did feel low in my mind. My mother told him that I was getting entirely out of hand and that he must give me a good whipping or I would break everything in the house besides making them all thoroughly miserable. Father said he was too prostrated to undertake the whipping then, but that he would attend to it after supper.

Supper was a doleful affair. I had never sat through such a nerve-wearing ordeal before. I was in the deepest disgrace and everybody, including little Florence, was sunk in woe. I had never been so thoroughly unhappy.

After supper my father announced that he would read his paper first, and when he had finished he would take up the whipping matter. I had never had a whipping. My mother had spanked me aplenty, but I did not regard that as a whipping. I wondered what it would be like to be whipped. I waited patiently until my father had finished his evening paper, sitting in a deep gloom meanwhile, but with no fear or terror. My woe was born of having broken my mother's pier glass, which she treasured, and of throwing the whole family into gloom.

When my father had finished his paper he got up briskly, saying, "Well now. Come along, Percy. Let's attend to this whipping business." He led the way out into the back yard where we visited my mother's shrubs and bushes, from which a suitable whip was to be cut. My father had his pocket knife open, ready to cut when he found a stalk that met the requirements. He explained to me that it was necessary to find one that had just the right length and thickness and straightness. If it were too short it would not have enough spring. If it were too long it would have too much spring and would break. If it were too thin it would be weak, whereas, if it were too thick it would bruise, which of course would not do.

We searched and searched without finding anything that just suited. I became interested in the problem and pointed out several likely-looking sticks which appeared as though they might answer the exacting specifications. He discussed my selections with me, examining each one with care. After spending quite a time at it, he finally decided that the best thing to do would be to cut several and try them. He cut a long thin one, a long thick one, a middle-length one, and several other compromises. This made five whips. I was very much impressed with his technique. I could see that between all of the whips it was more than likely that one would be found which would suit much better than possibly could be the case were one only to be selected by guessing. I did not recognize it at the time, but I had received my first lesson in engineering research.

After all had been prepared and whittled down smooth he said, "Now come along up to my room and we will try them." He led the way to the third-floor front, which was his room. Arrived here, he took off his coat, his collar, and necktie, and rolled up his sleeves. I was a bit concerned at this, for it suggested that a whipping must be something calling for considerable activity. He laid the five whips on the bed and, taking one at a time, he smote the coverlet. The savage whir and the succeeding whack sounded all over the house. He put real muscle into it. The long thin whip broke. He explained that he had expected this to happen, for the stick was too thin for its length. The thick one made a fearful whir and whack when it hit the coverlet. We rejected this one because it was evident that it would bruise. Later on I heard my mother say that she never suffered such horrible nervous strain in all her life, listening to the savage whir of the whip and the awful whack as it struck. She imagined my little body might be receiving these blows; but as I did not cry out and as she could hear me talking calmly afterward, she assumed that I could not be suffering very acutely. I firmly believe that most of this bed-whacking business was for my mother's benefit, as she sat downstairs trying to read.

When we had whacked the bed coverlet for a long

time, testing the whips and breaking most of them, my father was far from being satisfied. He sat down on the edge of the bed and outlined in his clear way the problem as it confronted us. Said he, "What we need is something fairly long, very strong, and yet very light. It also must be very springy. Where can we find such a thing which we could use for a whip?"

We thought and thought. By this time I was as keenly interested in the solution of the problem as though some one else were to receive the whipping. I suggested a baseball bat, but in the same breath I pointed out that it was unsuitable, although I pointed out that it would hit awful hard.

"Oh, *much* too hard," he replied. "Why, you could break a man's back with a baseball bat, and kill him." He recoiled at the suggestion of a baseball bat.

"I suppose a broomstick would be too stiff, too," I ventured.

"Altogether too stiff and too heavy. It would break bones and be very dangerous."

There was a long pause here while we both thought. Then an idea occurred to me. "Gosh, Papa! I know the very thing. That thin cane of yours." Among his walking-sticks was a very thin one which I used to admire.

"By Jove!" he exclaimed. "That's a good idea. Go and fetch it."

I remember hurrying downstairs to the clothes-closet in the butler's pantry where the canes and umbrellas were kept. As I ran through the reception-room, being in my usual hurry, I had to pass my mother. She seemed much surprised to see me hurrying to the clothes-closet. She asked me what I was after. I answered:

"We're trying to find a good whip. We're going to try the thin cane."

She asked something else, but I was much too busy to stop just then and explain. She afterward said that my being in such a hurry to find a cane with which to be whipped seemed one of the most extraordinary things she ever heard of.

When I returned with the thin cane my father whacked the coverlet with it with all his might. It made a particularly savage noise. My mother must have winced when she heard it. After whacking the bed coverlet until my mother was ready to fly out of her skin, my father shook his head and handed the cane to me, asking me to try it and say what I thought. I had noticed him putting a lot of "beef" into his blows, so I decided to put in all I had. Getting the best grip I could, which was difficult on account of the curved

[107]

handle, I whacked the bed coverlet for all that was in me. It only made a fair noise and my father feared my mother might not hear it. He told me to put more "beef" into it. I wiped off my hands, took a fresh grip, took careful aim, and belabored the coverlet with all my might. When my father expressed disappointment over the weight of my blows, I explained that the curved handle got in my way and that no one could hit hard, with the handle where it was. My father was not satisfied and we went into executive session again. It was quite apparent to me what was required, but we would have to do a lot of searching around to find just exactly the thing. It must have appeared this way to my father, too, for he finally said,

"Well, I guess we shall have to give up the whipping, Percy. We can't seem to find the right whip. But, anyway, you understand that you must be more careful around the house and that you must not make so much trouble for Mamma, don't you; and you will begin to-morrow morning and try to be a better boy, won't you, Percy?"

I was very deeply impressed by the way he said it. He was asking me as a favor to him and to Mamma to do something. I realized that it would be very mean indeed of me to fail to do as he asked. And it would be yet meaner not to try to make things more pleasant for Mamma. So I said, "Yes, Papa. I will." And then we went downstairs and explained to Mamma that the whipping matter had to be called off. I am glad to be able to say that I kept my promise in pretty fair shape, as time proved.

§7

I cannot imagine what led my father to do such a foolish thing, but on one occasion about this time he took little Florence along when he and I went crabbing near Coney Island. Fishing for blue crabs was one of his favorite pastimes. I went with him frequently. He used to bring the crabs home and have them boiled and we ate them. My mother was never impressed favorably by the crabs. She insisted that they tasted of kerosene oil. I agreed. But I did not acknowledge it, because my father loved the crabs and I wanted him to feel that we loved them too.

When we went crabbing we used to hire a rowboat in the little river which makes Coney Island an island, and row to a place where we could anchor or tie up to something. We would then tie three or four chunks of raw meat to lines and lower them overboard to the bottom. Each would be left down five minutes or so. Then, one at a time, I would pull them up very slowly. When they were near the surface we could see from one to six crabs eating the meat. My father would then scoop the whole business up in a net and empty it in the bottom of the boat. The crabs would be very indignant, and would scuttle around on the bottom of the boat, looking for whoever was to blame for their predicament. A freshly caught big blue crab is about as belligerent a creature as I know.

Of all enterprises on which to embark with my sister Florence, a crab-fishing expedition seemed to me the most ill-advised. I knew Florence and what a small thing could send her into screaming hysterics. But she was taken along, for what reason passed my understanding.

She was only a little girl, probably about four years of age, and she was very talkative as she walked along, her hand in her father's, on the way from the horse car to the boat. I suspect she may have been bragging that she was not afraid of crabs. My father assured her they were nice little creatures and would not eat little girls. But Florence had no idea what six or eight of them scuttling around on the bottom of a small rowboat would be like. I knew what they were like; how one had to hold his feet up in the air until the crabs had settled down. My father did not know so much about her as I did; but I thought it best to say nothing.

When we arrived at the boat, all my father's powers of persuasion were needed to get her into it. She held on very tightly, and carried a look of profound disapproval on her little face as my father rowed out from shore. I fancy it was her first experience in a rowboat.

But Florence was becoming adjusted to the new experience by the time we tied up and cast the baited lines overboard. I itched to get a good big haul—a whole scoop-net full of crabs—so that, when they were dumped on the bottom of the boat, Florence would be treated to a real show. I urged my father to leave the lines a long time. I believed this would attract more crabs. Finally his patience became exhausted and he told me to go ahead and pull up a line. He grasped the scoop-net and prepared for action. Florence became intensely interested. I pulled in very gently, so as not to scare off a single crab from the bait. Then my father wielded the scoop-net; and telling Florence she was about to see some lovely little crabs, dumped the contents of the net on the bottom of the boat.

Instantly some six or eight large blue crabs declared war and began scuttling furiously, claws held aloft. Some of them came my way and I lifted my feet and squealed with mock fright. Some approached my father's feet and he kicked them away, the crabs making savage bites at his shoes. Still others headed directly for Florence. It was too much for her. Holding up her feet as high as she could get them, she opened her mouth and let go a series of shrieks that brought the entire countryside to attention. People stopped what they were doing and stared at us; others stuck their heads up out of small boats and peered at us suspiciously. For once in his life my father was thoroughly embarrassed. He tried to calm Florence. But Florence was beyond being calmed. He finally took her in his arms. I was outraged; I could have slapped her.

After a long time and a lot of talking, explaining, and persuading my father got Florence where she would sit away back on the stern seat of the boat beside him, with her feet doubled up under her, where the crabs could not reach her. Then to show her that a crab might be ever so ugly and yet need not be permitted to come near, he prodded one with the handle of the scoop-net. It fought the handle as a crab will, and he succeeded in getting the child where she could look at a crab without out screaming. It really was a masterful effort on his part, for little Florence was very self-willed. Most people would have taken such a child ashore and gone home. But not my father.

After a while he told me to pull up another line, talking to Florence meanwhile and explaining to her just what was going on, how he was going to catch some more crabs and when we had enough we were going to take them home and cook and eat them. He scooped another netful and had her watch how he emptied it. She recoiled as the crabs started scuttling, for her nature revolted at such sights. However, she held on to herself and did not scream.

When we had caught what my father thought was enough he gathered them into a bag and we started for home. As we walked to the horse-car line he asked her why she had screamed. She replied, "I don't like crabs very well. Did you see that one fighting with himself?" For many years we used to quote, "Did you see that one fighting with himself?" As my father pointed out, it's exactly what a crab seems to be doing.

§ 8

When Florence had been at school long enough to begin arithmetic, something happened and she could not go on. The child appeared unable to grasp what it was the teacher wanted her to do. Possibly it was the combination of a stupid and unimaginative teacher and an intensely imaginative and high-strung child.

After this difficulty had continued for some time, my mother was requested to call at the school to talk about her daughter's standing. The teacher informed my mother that Florence had exhibited a total inability to understand arithmetic. Manifestly the child was defective mentally. If there be one thing which a mother will not believe it is that her child is defective mentally. When she heard this, the fire entered my mother's eye and the iron entered her soul. She said she would take her daughter home, have a talk with her, and bring her back to school. She served notice she would show all concerned that it was somebody other than her daughter who was mentally defective.

That evening, when my father returned from business, my mother unburdened her soul. "A child of mine defective mentally!" my father snorted. He was for going over to the school and cleaning out the entire place. There was a long conference during which my mother got it across to my indignant father that the trouble had been with arithmetic, and if he would take a hand in the matter Florence might be brought out of her difficulty. He had pulled me out of a terrible difficulty which I had encountered in long division and long multiplication. He had made it such a fascinating pastime that I used to divide enormous numbers by other enormous numbers just for the fun of doing it. The conference ended by his saying, "Let me have a talk with Florence after supper."

After supper he inveigled Florence into some sort of

conversation about games and puzzles. I suspected this might be the beginning of something interesting, so I hung around. He suddenly directed his conversation at me, which was disconcerting until I realized he was talking at Florence through me. Finally he said:

"I say, Florence, you ought to be the kind that enjoys arithmetic. You have such a clear mind that you would be good at it. It's lots of fun when you play it the right way. Do you have arithmetic at your school?"

Florence was not enthusiastic. She indicated that they had arithmetic at her school but she did not like it.

"Oh well, if you don't like it then they are not playing it right. Let me show you how we used to play it when I was a boy down in Maine. Percy, go down to the kitchen and fetch me a handful of beans."

This was enough for me. Something big was in the wind. I fetched the beans in a jiffy.

"Now, Florence, I'm going to play arithmetic with Percy first. After you see how we play it I shall play it with you, because I know you would play it better than most people. You are much smarter than most children of your age."

He placed ten beans in a vertical row on a sheet of paper. He then asked me to add up the beans and write down how many there were. I ran up the row and counted ten.

"All right," said he. "You have added up all the beans and you find there are ten. Draw a line at the bottom and write down ten, so we won't be forgetting it."

I drew a line and wrote down "10."

"All right. That's easy, of course. Anybody can do that. Now I am going to make it a little harder."

He then laid down on the paper in a vertical row five groups of two beans each. "Draw your line and add those up," said he. I started to count them up one at a time, but he stopped me, saying, "Oh no. That's too easy. You must add the piles. Two and two make four, four and two make six, six and two make eight —like that."

I caught the idea, so I added, "Two and two make four, four and two make six, six and two make eight, eight and two make ten." I drew my line and wrote down "10." I was becoming interested.

"By Jove! Mamma," he called to my mother, "but these are a couple of smart children. You ought to see them add by arithmetic."

He then laid out on the paper three groups of three beans each and one lone bean. "Now add up those beans," he said. I drew my line and added, "Three and three make six, six and three make nine, nine and one make ten." I wrote down "10." Florence was getting interested by this time. I saw that she was getting an entirely new slant on arithmetic, as indeed I was also.

"Oh well, we shall catch him yet, shan't we, Florence?"

Florence's response to this was a grunt. Next he arranged two groups of four beans each and one little group of two beans. "Let's see you add that one up." I had the scheme by this time, so I rattled off, "Four and four make eight, eight and two make ten."

"Well, well. This is wonderful! But let's see you do this one." He then arranged two groups of five beans each on the paper, one over the other. I saw the answer before he had his beans arranged, so I added, "Five and five make ten." I wondered what he was going to do next. The end of his scheme seemed to have been reached. He took six beans and grouped them and then took four more beans and grouped them. Without being asked I added, "Six and four make ten."

"Let me do it now, Papa," interrupted Florence.

This was exactly what he had been playing for, but he was not going to let her into the game too easily. "Let Percy and me finish," he said.

He must have slipped another bean into his hand at this juncture, for he laid down one group of seven beans and over this a group of four. I had not noticed that he had smuggled in an extra bean. Before he had

[117]

the beans arranged I started adding, "Seven and three make ——"

"No, no," exclaimed Florence, her eyes flashing with indignation. "There are four beans there! That makes one more. *Eleven!*" she shouted at me, intent upon beating me to the answer. "It's eleven, isn't it, Papa?"

"Eleven?" my father questioned, as though surprised. "It always has been ten," and he winked at me.

Florence had her eyes on the beans and did not see the wink. "It's eleven beans, Papa. Don't you see? There are seven in that pile and four in that one."

"But we only had ten beans. How can it be eleven? It must be ten."

Florence was sure, and when Florence was sure that ended it.

"Papa!" she insisted. "Don't you see seven beans in that pile?"

"Yes, Florence, I see them."

"Well, don't you see four beans in that pile?" pointing to the smaller pile.

"Yes, Florence, I see them."

"Well, Papa, how many beans are there all together? Count them."

He counted the seven group one at a time and continued with the four group, ending up with eleven. He seemed to be completely mystified. Little Florence, her

[118]

piercing eyes on his face, awaited his comprehension. But comprehension did not seem to come.

"Don't you understand, Papa?" she queried, with a touch of impatience at his slowness. Hesitatingly, he repeated, "Seven and four make—" He appeared to be stuck fast, and unable to go on.

"Eleven," Florence prompted. "Can't you understand, Papa?" It was she who was giving the lesson in arithmetic now.

He removed one bean from the four group, as though struggling with the problem.

"That's ten now," she exclaimed, "because there are only three in that pile now."

"I guess you must be right, Florence, but let's go on." Florence shifted her stand and cast a bored look at me which said, "Gee! But he's stupid."

Then he laid out eight beans in one group and two in the other. Both Florence and I shouted at the top of our lungs, "Eight and two make ten." While we were saying it, he dropped another bean in the two bean group. Instantly Florence and I corrected ourselves, shouting louder than ever, "Eight and three make eleven." But before we could get it out of our mouths he slipped two more beans into the smaller pile. Florence and I stared at each other as we struggled to be first in performing the mental feat of adding two more beans. It was a dead heat. We shouted in concert, "Eight and five make thirteen!"

It is not necessary to rehearse here how he led little Florence into adding up all sorts of combinations, gradually shifting into subtraction without her realizing it. We played the game all the evening, he being clever enough to keep changing it so that our interest was not allowed to flag. My mother finally had to stop us so that Florence might go to bed.

The next day Florence was taken back to school by my mother. I do not know what happened then, though I can easily imagine that some additional and quite positive statements were made about her not being defective mentally; but I do know that from that day on, until finally Florence graduated from a four-year course at high school, she stood number one in every one of her classes, except on three or four occasions when she slipped and had to accept number two. When she had to accept second place she considered herself disgraced. It used to require the united efforts of the entire family to lift her out of her gloom.

None of us ever found out what happened in Florence's mind to cause this remarkable shift. I think I knew her better than did any one and I have always believed that the clever manipulation by my father straightened out some sort of preconceived notion which had been holding her back. What the teacher thought had happened to the "mental defective" is not known to history.

§9

One April Fool's Day a boy brought to my school at Hoyt and President Streets a paper bag containing a few chocolate caramels, which looked particularly inviting as one peered down into the bag. At recess he was surprisingly generous with them. I never knew such generosity as this boy displayed. Ordinarily, if a boy had any candy, it was cheap taffy. In a crowd of boys he was careful to keep to himself the fact that he had any. He might take into his confidence one or two very close friends, in which case they would repair to some unfrequented spot where the taffy would be divided and devoured. But this boy broke all precedents by exhibiting the bag and its contents in public.

He was surrounded immediately by a clamoring mob. Backing up against a fence, where he could keep his eye on everybody, he held the crowd at bay while he selected those who were to be favored. I pushed into the crowd, hoping that by some lucky turn one of the candies might come my way. He had given out four or five of them, and they were being enthusiastically sucked, when one of the boys executed a wild maneuver and spat out his caramel. The crowd had not made up its mind what to think about this astonishing proceeding when another boy gave a yell, spat out his caramel, and made a break for the drinking-water. The others followed in short order. In a moment the crowd was in a hilarious uproar. The word was quickly passed around that the candies, instead of being caramels, were cubes of laundry soap coated with chocolate.

The owner of these interesting candies became a hero at once. He had fooled the whole crowd. My soul was filled with admiration for him. For the remainder of the recess I did nothing but feast my eyes upon him. It seemed to me that he was possessed of every admirable human attribute. His initiative in securing the candies, the nice clean white paper bag which added such a convincing touch, the cleverness of the idea of chocolate-coated soap, his boldness in carrying the offensive straight to the howling mob single-handed, his leadership as he selected his favored ones and bestowed his gifts—all reflected greatness. I never could have done it. One must have been a boy and have attended a large public school to appreciate this boy's courage.

When we reconvened in our classes I could think of nothing else. The thought came to me that it would be a brilliant stroke to work one of these soap candies off on my father. He had played jokes on me ever since I could remember; here was my chance to play one on him. I resolved to negotiate for one of the candies and to put through the joke on my father.

In those days, and I suppose it is the same today, it was a serious misdemeanor to send notes during class. But to be sure of getting one of the soap caramels I must put in my application early, or they might all be given away, or sat upon, or squeezed, or partly melted. I decided to risk a note. I wrote out on a scrap of paper: "Please save me one candy. Very important." Incidentally, I remember being quite proud of that word "important." I rolled up the bit of paper, and catching Will's eye, indicated that the paper ball was for him. It was passed along under cover of the desks and reached him. He unrolled it, read it, and nodded his agreement. The dreadful ordeal was over.

After school I sought him out. I told him I dearly wanted a soap caramel to work on my father, but it must be a perfect one.

"Your father!" he exclaimed.

"Yes," I replied, adding, "he's always working jokes on me and I want to pay him back."

"Gee, Percy! I wouldn't dare work one on my father; but you can go ahead and work yours if you want to."

He was beginning to admire my courage. He opened his paper bag, selected the best-looking piece of candy, and gave it to me. I thought it mighty kind of him. He was a hero and I was nothing but one of a crowd.

I wrapped the precious object in my handkerchief and went directly home, so that by no chance could anything happen to it during the afternoon, when everything from the soles of my feet to the top of my head would get bumped and squeezed and knocked very thoroughly. I secreted the candy pending that half hour after supper when the family would be gathered in the reception-room.

That evening at supper I could eat only with the greatest difficulty. After dinner I was terribly nervous. Unwrapping my treasure, I walked over to my father, who had begun to read his paper, and said in my most ingratiating tone, holding out the soap caramel, "Papa, would you like a piece of candy?"

My father gave me a penetrating glance and then looked hard at the candy. There was a painful pause of a few seconds, during which, in all probability, his lightning-like mind canvassed the possibilities. I suppose my face, together with the irregularity of the entire proceeding, aroused his suspicions. But he was too clever to disclose it to me. "Why, yes, Percy. Thank you." And he took the soap caramel and put it in his mouth, at least as far as I could see. He began working on it as one does on a piece of candy.

I returned to my chair behind him and awaited the explosion. I had my boisterous laugh all ready for the moment when he arrived at the soap. I pictured him bolting for the sink in the butler's pantry to spit it out, and I could contain myself only with the greatest effort. The moments passed and nothing happened. I became concerned. Surely, enough time had gone by for him to have sucked off the chocolate. But not a sign from him.

After several minutes, during which I never removed my gaze from him, I moved around to where I could see his face. He was not moving his mouth. He must have finished it. Discovering me looking at him, he glanced up from his paper as though waiting for me to speak. Since he expected something from me, I asked, "Did you like it, Papa?"

"Yes, Percy, very much. Have you any more of them?"

"No. I haven't any more of them," I answered, completely set back.

I returned to my chair deeply crestfallen. I did not know what to think. Could it have been a good candy I gave him? I could not make up my mind, and to this day I have no idea whether it really was a good candy, or whether, suspecting me from the start, he had only pretended to put it in his mouth and suck on it, but had really secreted it in his hand. Or finally, whether he actually ate it, soap and all. I never quite liked to ask him about it. He took his secret with him to his grave, many years after.

§ 10

I may have been eight or nine years of age when my father and I were standing in the doorway of the old Fifth Avenue Hotel in New York, watching a passing parade. The parade was in honor of the great American of the day, General Ulysses S. Grant. There was a crowd out on the pavement, but at one side of the doorway there was an open space, and my father and I could see better from there than in the crowd. A portly, white-haired, rather distinguished-looking gentleman with a very red face was the only other occupant of this space.

The parade had been going on for some time, when the portly gentleman turned to my father and, in a voice which appeared to be very badly blurred, remarked, "Great man—Gennel Grann."

My father turned quickly and eyed the speaker narrowly for what seemed an embarrassing interval. His eyes were very dark brown and very piercing, and he had a quick, nervous, intense manner about him, quite unlike anybody else in all the world except his brothers. After eyeing the portly gentleman, he turned away as though to ignore him; but quickly returning his gaze, he ejaculated, in his characteristic and sudden way,

"What's that, sir?"

"I shed great man—Gennel Grann."

"Oh!" replied my father. "Yes indeed." There was a pause, the portly man meanwhile eyeing my father steadily and critically. "Let's see. Who did you say it was, sir?" asked my father.

"Gennel Grann," answered the portly man.

"General Grant?" repeated my father, as though trying to remember where he had heard the name.

"Didger never hear of Gennel Grann, sir?" the portly man returned, looking at my father belligerently.

"It seems to me I have—somewhere. Let me see. Seems to me I've read something about him in the newspapers recently."

"D'yer mean to say, sir, you doan' know who Gennel Grann is?"

"I suppose it's very stupid of me, but you know, sir, I cannot just recall him for the moment. What did he do?"

"What did Gennel Grann do!"

[127]

"Oh! Just a moment. It's coming to me now. He wrote some very beautiful poetry, did he not, sir?"

"Oouch-h-h!" cried the portly man, getting more red in the face than ever. "Gennel Grann write poetry! Oouch-h-h!" Then very severely to my father: "Gennel Grann's a shouldier, sir. Great shouldier. Great man. Wonnerful great man 'n' shouldier, sir."

"Really! What did he do?" inquired my father, as if tremendously impressed.

"Gennel Grann?" exclaimed the portly man, in sheer amazement.

"Yes, sir. What did he do?"

"D'yer mean to shay, sir, you doan' know about Gennel Grann?"

"I don't believe I do, sir. Do you?"

"Oouch-h-h! Shay, sir, d'yer ever hear of Abraham Lincoln?"

"I think I have heard the name, sir."

"Oouch-h-h! D'yer ever hear of George Washington?"

"I don't think I ever did, sir."

"Oouch-h-h! He never heard of George Washington! Where you been all your life, sir? Shay! D'yer ever hear of Julius Cæsar?"

"Oh yes! I've heard of Julius Cæsar. He's an actor or something, isn't he? He acts with Edwin Booth, seems to me."

A policeman happened along at this point. The red-faced man beckoned to him.

"Offisher," declared the red-faced one, "here's a man never heard of Julius Cæsar, or George Washington, or Abraham Lincoln, or Gennel Grann! Offisher, y'oughter lock him up."

The policeman smiled an indulgent smile, looked at my father, who winked, and remarked that he thought maybe he'd better; but in the meantime he advised that the portly gentleman go inside and sit down and cool off, as he might get hurt out on the sidewalk in such a crowd. My father and I watched while the policeman assisted him inside the hotel and sat him down on a sofa. We saw him sputtering and shaking his head indignantly as long as we were there.

§ 11

On another occasion, when my father and I were returning from some sort of an expedition, he dropped into a very ornate barroom for a glass of beer. I had been there many times with him. I was always deeply impressed by what I took to be a very beautiful painting which hung on the wall at the end of this barroom. It showed a very genial bearded gentleman in a brilliant red cloak astride a huge barrel and holding aloft a tankard of very foamy beer. The brilliant red cloak was stunning, in my judgment. I asked my father who the man in the picture was supposed to be. Glancing at it in a bored way, he answered, "Oh, that's the man who invented lager beer."

This answer satisfied my thirst for information, seemed logical, and gave me something to think about.

Awhile later, my mother and my father and I and some friends were strolling through a picture-gallery. I believe it was the Metropolitan Art Museum in New York. We were in the gallery devoted to religious pictures and happened to pause before one in which there was a man in a brilliant red cloak. Pointing to it, I piped up, "Look, Mamma. I know who that is."

Proud of her son's knowledge of art, she asked me who it was. In a shrill voice which is said to have penetrated the entire room, I answered, "That's the man who invented lager beer." My mother was shocked. She hurried me out of the room; my father followed, laughing so heartily that he had to wipe his eyes.

§ 12

One of the great troubles which pursued my father day and night was absent-mindedness. He insisted upon losing umbrellas, packages, books, drawings, etc., until finally he became desperate. He could not cure himself of it. In his characteristic way he once sought my sympathy. I was only a little boy, but all my life he had treated me as an equal, so that it was entirely natural for him to come to me for sympathy.

On this occasion he happened to be in the mood to talk to me. He held his head in his hands as he sat on the back stoop, sighed like a blast furnace, and remarked that he believed he would burst out crying. This used to concern me deeply. I had no desire to see him burst out crying. Something told me it would not be a pleasant spectacle. I had never seen him cry. I could not imagine such a terrible thing happening. I did not want it. And so I sought to console him.

"What makes you feel like crying, Papa?" I asked.

"Oh, nobody loves me, nobody cares about me, nobody helps me, everybody is cross with me when I lose my things."

This was very terrible, it seemed to me. Unless I cheered him up I could see that we would both be in tears.

"We all love you, Papa. Mamma does, and I do, and Florence does, and Addie will when she gets old enough."

"Yes, but that doesn't stop me from losing my things. Yesterday I lost my gloves. Today I lost a roll of drawings."

"Well, why don't you hold them in your hand, Papa? That's the way I do when I want to be sure not to lose what I have. I just hang right on to it all the time, and never put it down until I get home. Then I know I can't lose it."

"But the trouble is, I forget and I put it down, and then I walk away without it."

I had to admit that this was a difficult problem. If he could not remember to hold his things in his hands, it seemed very baffling.

"Well, Papa, could you remember just one thing— just one single thing to do always?"

"I wonder if I could. What would it be, Percy?"

"It seems to me that if you had a piece of paper with your name on it, and if you could remember to put it on everything when you first pick it up, then when you lost it somebody would find it and know that you lost it and send it to you."

"Well, now, Percy! That's an idea. You see, I could have a lot of little paper stickers printed with my name and address on them, and if I carried them in my pocketbook and could remember to stick them on everything that I picked up, when I lost anything the one who found it would know who had lost it."

He was surprised and immensely pleased at my having exhibited enough imagination to formulate a solution of a baffling problem. He was so impressed with my idea that he had stickers printed. I remember them clearly. They were somewhat larger than a modern special-delivery stamp, and they had a red margin around them and bore the interesting legend:

THIS WAS LOST BY A DAMNED FOOL NAMED

HIRAM STEVENS MAXIM

WHO LIVES AT 325 UNION STREET, BROOKLYN.

A SUITABLE REWARD WILL BE PAID FOR

ITS RETURN.

He used these stickers until everything we owned seemed to have one stuck on it. My mother finally lost her patience and vetoed their further use.

§ 13

One of my father's brothers visited us while we were in Union Street. I am quite sure it was his brother Hudson. These two were a pair. Each one encouraged the other to more and more bizarre performances. What one did not think of, the other did. Uncle Hudson contracted the toothache while he was with us. My mother provided all manner of hot applications, including oil of cloves and the usual run of old-fashioned home remedies, most of which depended upon superstition or hypnosis of the sufferer, according to my father.

[133]

There were not so many dentists as there are now. People either did not have so much trouble with their teeth or they permitted them to take care of themselves. And thus it was Uncle Hudson never thought of going to a dentist.

He went over to New York with my father every day. His visit may have been something like a fortnight. During this entire visit the toothache was troubling Uncle Hudson. Each night something different was done by my mother. My father paid no attention; such details bored him, if they did not trouble him directly.

And so the days came and went, Uncle Hudson bothering every night with his toothache, and my sympathetic little mother doing everything in her power to alleviate his suffering. One night it became very painful indeed, and Uncle Hudson was driven to pacing the floor with a hot cloth on his face. This went on for an hour or more, my father doing his utmost to keep his mind free from Uncle Hudson's trouble. But there came a time when my father's patience became exhausted. While my mother was in the kitchen warming something for Uncle Hudson, and while I was thought to be out of hearing, which I was not, my father, in exasperation, said:

"Gawd, Ike! You're driving me crazy with your

toothache." My father always called Uncle Hudson "Ike."

"It's a terrible pity about you. The top of my head's coming off."

"Well, I'll tell you what to do. It's what I did when I had the toothache. Hunt up a horse doctor or a good blacksmith or a dentist, have the tooth pulled out, put it down on the floor and let the damned thing *ache*!"

That is precisely what Uncle Hudson had to do finally.

§ 14

It must have been when we first returned to Brooklyn, when I was between seven and eight, that my mother and one of her friends took me to a matinée at Booth's Theater on Twenty-third Street in New York. I remember the inside of the theater very well. We had seats away down front, very close to the stage. My mother's friend, a Mrs. Drake, sat inside; my mother came next; and I sat on the aisle seat. I had never been to a theater before. As might be imagined, I was profoundly impressed. The action on the stage was absolutely real to me. The play had a lot to do with Indians, my pet horror. I was too young to grasp much beyond the fact that the men and women on the stage

were in dreadful trouble on account of the approach of
the Indians. I was stunned by the awful situation. I
had thought about such a frightful thing happening.
Here I was plunged right in the middle of the reality.

I could not divorce myself from the people on the
stage. There they were, not twenty-five feet away, talking and worrying about the coming of the Indians. If
they were in such dire straits, the same thing applied
to me, my mother, and Mrs. Drake. I sat on the edge of
my seat, my hands clenched in agony, the cold sweat
pouring out of me, wondering what possibly could be
done about the situation. I could not escape the thought
that the wise thing to do was to start running now,
while the way was clear. The street was handy and there
would be policemen out there. In fact, I saw a policeman at the door of the theater when we came in.

I nudged my mother and whispered that we had better get out into the street. She seemed perfectly at ease,
and whispered back something about its being very exciting, which seemed to me to be a very silly point of
view to take of such a serious situation. I continued to
sit on the edge of my seat, my eyes starting from their
sockets. The agony was fearfully long drawn out. The
people on the stage were a weak lot, for not one of
them did anything to protect himself. When one of
them thought he saw an Indian coming, and everybody

on the stage started running and screaming, I gave a terrible jump, my nerves being on edge. I thought the fatal hour had struck. I slid off my seat and made a grab for my mother's hand, fully intending to drag her out to the street, because I had no confidence in her running abilities. Mothers never are much good at running. But she caught hold of me and shook me, telling me that I positively must sit still and be quiet and not disturb the other people. She appeared to be struggling to restrain her laughter, which seemed to me very odd. In telling of this incident later she said that my face, as I watched the action on the stage, my eyes popping, my mouth open, worry written all over me, was one of the most appealing pictures she ever beheld.

At the time I seriously questioned my mother's judgment. The Indians were coming unquestionably. Everybody knew it. The people on the stage were talking about it that very moment. Why hang around? Why not take time by the forelock and get out into the street *now*? I made up my mind to explain the seriousness of the situation to her. I nudged her again and indicated I wanted to whisper in her ear. She bent down and I said, "I think we'd better get out in the street now, Mamma, before the Indians get here." To my astonishment she smiled and shook her head, motioning me to be quiet. I had done my best; I could not seem to impress the woman with the importance of getting going *now*.

Just as I feared, we waited too long. Amid the most nerve-shattering screaming and confusion I had ever experienced, the Indians came pouring in from the right-hand side of the stage. One look was enough for me. The tocsin had sounded! The time to act had come! With a bound, I fetched the aisle and started for the street, shouting to my mother at the very top of my lungs, "Come on, Mamma!"

Halfway up the aisle I turned to see how she was making out. She was coming, so I ran ahead and succeeded in reaching the door of the theater in safety. When she came out I was overcome with surprise to find that she was cross with me. She spoke seriously, told me I had broken up the performance and made it very unpleasant for everybody, especially for her; that they were not real Indians, but, instead, were ordinary men dressed up as Indians; that it was all make-believe; that everybody was pretending, just as children pretend when they play. It was a brand-new idea to me. I thought the entire affair was as real as anything I ever saw in all my life. She waited until the end of the act and then took me back to my seat, amid the amused glances of those about us. I was considerably reassured when I realized that no one seemed to have been tomahawked or killed and most of the people in the theater were looking at me and smiling. I had "stolen the show" for a few minutes, as it would be expressed today.

§ 15

My father was very even-tempered, in spite of his temperamental ways. There was only one thing that I can remember that really would make him cross. This was what he called "disorganization in the writing-materials department." Almost everything calculated to arouse irritability—from squalling children to smashed pier glasses—occurred in our house, and he, like the rest of us, was nervous and high strung; yet I cannot remember any irritability or fault-finding except when something went wrong with the supply of note-paper, envelopes, pens, ink, and blotter.

Every once in a while he would be moved to write a letter. One never knew when the urge would strike him. My mother seemed to be responsible for everything in our house. She did her best, poor dear, but no matter how often she put things in order in the drawer of the writing desk, they were sure to be out of order when my father wanted to write a letter. I blush to admit that I was the cause.

The writing-desk was in the little reception-room.

Every time I wanted a finely pointed tool with which to pick something, the only instrument I could think of which was available to me was the pen. Nine times out of ten I would bend or break the pen point. There were seldom other pens, because every so often I used to get all of them out, coat them with oil, magnetize them with my horseshoe magnet, and use them as little boats in the large silver waiter which stood at my mother's place at the dining-room table. My own wife has used this identical silver waiter for the past thirty-five years. My father had shown me how to play with magnetized pen points, using this waiter. On rainy afternoons it was my favorite pastime. By placing in the waiter enough water to give a depth of about a quarter of an inch, and by the proper use of the horseshoe magnet, the little pens, which would float by virtue of the oil on them, could be made to sail around in the most interesting fashion. The pens had enough temper in them to be permanent magnets once they were magnetized; this caused the bows of all "boats" to repel each other, all sterns to repel each other, but all bows to seek all sterns. Likewise, the bows would be repelled by one pole of the horseshoe magnet and be attracted by the other pole. As may be imagined, it was an ideal combination for a rainy afternoon; but a very bad thing for the writing-materials department. The pen points which were not broken were lost or forgotten. In any case they never seem to have found their way back to the drawer of the desk.

Frequently the entire penholder would be missing. I was responsible for this also. It was long and thin and stiff, and thus suited a multitude of purposes, such as substituting for a lost king bolt in my wagon, or serving as an axle for a small wheelbarrow, or plugging a hole in something. It always was broken, misplaced, or forgotten.

The ink was the only paint I had. Everything which needed to be colored had to be colored with this ink. The ink-bottle was the most detestable object in my young life. It would get tipped over in spite of every precaution. When the painting job was a big one, all the ink would be used. If this did not occur, then it got spilled when the wretched bottle tipped over. If neither of these occurred, then I intended to put it back, but forgot to do so in my perpetual hurry.

The blotters were utterly impossible to keep. No matter how many my mother bought, there never were any in the drawer. They were used in quantity when the miserable ink-bottle tipped over, and also for a wide variety of drying jobs. Blotters were indispensable in my daily operations. Envelopes were hard to keep on hand, also. They acted as convenient receptacles for all manner of things. When I needed one I needed it badly and in a great hurry. I did not use much of the note-paper; it could be used for home work from school, but I detested home work, and so the demand was not heavy.

Thus it may be judged that when my father decided he must write a letter, the writing-materials in the drawer of the writing-desk were usually in a state of demoralization. He went through a regular set program when he discovered this. First, he would be found scratching around in the drawer of the writing-desk like a squirrel, emitting grunts. This would develop into an appeal to the Almighty to look down and bear witness to the fact that there was no pen, although less than a week ago he had been to the stationer's shop and had laid in a complete supply of everything. And here he was faced with the fact that every snitch of the pens had been used. After pawing everything topsy-turvy he would slam the drawer shut, lift both arms to heaven, and with a fervor that would have brought tears to the eyes of a wooden Indian he would cry through his clenched teeth, "O my gawd!"

This over, he would tramp upstairs, seeking my mother, hissing and groaning on the way. My mother always seemed to be upstairs doing something to a baby. He would almost break down over the writing-materials.

When he had announced their depletion he would gesticulate, pace up and down the floor, apparently tear his hair, and take on in a manner which would frighten one not accustomed to it. This would continue until my mother was through with the baby, when the two of them would go downstairs, she leading the way and he apostrophizing Heaven as he followed her, referring constantly to the enormous supply of writing-materials he had purchased the previous week.

When they arrived at the writing-desk, the chances were about even that one or more of the essentials to the writing of a letter would be missing. If they were, he would pace the floor, tear at his hair, hiss the most diabolical sentiments through his clenched teeth, and finally clap his hat upon his head and stride out the door on his way to the stationer's, where he would stock up with a fresh supply of everything.

I suppose that I must have witnessed this little scene a great many times. An outsider would have expected to see murder done the next moment; but in the family no one paid much attention to these fits. I am sure he enjoyed throwing them. It gave him an opportunity to blow off steam and he realized that he was throwing a fit as few persons are able to. I would have enjoyed hugely watching him throw his fits, had it not been for the fact that I was to blame for the entire trouble.

When he would return from the stationer's, having grossly over-purchased, as I do invariably, he would be in normal equable temper, and would sit down and write his letter as quietly and pleasantly as any one could wish.

PART IV

WAYNE, MAINE, AND BROOKLYN

As far back as my memory goes I was taken at irregular intervals to Wayne, Maine, where my father's parents had come to live. My consecutive memory of Wayne begins when I was sent there alone from Brooklyn when I was about nine. It was as crazy a thing to do as could be imagined, starting a boy of nine alone on a trip from New York to Winthrop, Maine, the nearest railroad station to Wayne. My mother fought the idea tooth and nail, but she had her husband and her son against her, for I was keen to go. I knew so little about the practical things which were involved that I could not see anything but the excitement of going. She finally yielded under protest, probably because of my coaxing as much as anything. My father insisted that as long as I had "an English tongue in my head" I could find my way. That was a very wrong premise.

I had a vague idea I would be placed on a Fall River line boat at New York and on a train at the place where the boat stopped; that Mr. and Mrs. Haynes would take me off the train at Boston and look after me for a day or so; that they would put me on another train in due time, and that there was something about getting off this train and taking another train which would take me to Winthrop, where Uncle Sam would meet me and drive me to Wayne. But all of this was boring detail to me. I did not bother my head about it.

My first awakening, and it was a rude one, occurred when I was taken to my quarters on the Fall River boat by my father and mother, and the time came for them to go ashore and leave me. I shall never forget to the last day of my life the sickening sensation when I awoke to what it meant to be left alone to shift for myself. They kissed me good-by and waited on the dock for the boat to back out into the stream. As I stood and watched my mother's tear-dimmed eyes, as the boat sailed away and she receded into the distance, the greatest sadness which had ever come to me in my nine years of life welled up within me. The tears came and I sought my bunk and cried as I had never cried before. It was several hours before I could even partially control myself. If ever a boy was low in his mind, I was that boy. The stewardess had been asked to look after me and several times she visited me and tried to comfort me; but I was broken-hearted, and would have sacrificed gladly anything on earth to have been able to

lay my head on my mother's breast and feel her arms
about me.

The night on the boat is all a hazy jumble of torture
in my memory. I must have been placed on the Boston
train at Fall River, but I have no recollection of it, probably being too depressed and too sleepy for impressions
to register.

I think I remember being turned over to Mr. Haynes
by the train conductor when the train reached Boston.
I clearly remember that Mr. and Mrs. Haynes were
very kind to me and that they bought me a little steamboat. It had an alcohol lamp in it, and Mr. Haynes
helped me get up steam and run it in a pond in Boston
Common. My spirits revived in Boston because I knew
there was someone who would look out for me.

Mr. Haynes put me on the Portland train in due
course. I have a hazy memory of subsequently walking
down a platform with my hand in that of a kindly conductor and of being placed in another train. I imagine
this must have been at Portland, where one has to
change cars to proceed farther north. I also remember
being on the lookout for the station where I had seen a
cage of bears when I had been to Maine before with my
parents. The train reached this station and I had a good
look at the bears. Some eight years ago—which would
be forty-six years since I had seen the station with the

bears—I was passing through Maine and I resolved to watch for the station where they used to have the bears. In due time we came to it and I remembered it distinctly. The bears were gone, and the cage, but the grass plots were there and the track arrangement and the general layout were just as I remembered them. If I am not mistaken the place was Lewiston.

My Uncle Sam met me at Winthrop and all was well. I had recovered from my low spirits, although that dear tear-dimmed face on the dock at New York made a lump come in my throat whenever I thought of it. Uncle Sam let me drive the horse part of the way to Wayne. And thus began nearly two months of unrestrained country life with my grandfather, grandmother, and Uncle Sam.

One day I took a walk with my grandfather. He seemed to be the oldest man I had ever seen in my life. We met another man and, to my amazement, he looked older than my grandfather. I had not believed such a thing possible.

"Hiram Percy Maxim," said my grandfather to me, "this gentleman used to be my school-teacher." (My father's people invariably called me by my full name.)

I was very much impressed, and after the old gentleman had gone I said to my grandfather, "How old are you, Grandpa?"

"How old would you think, Hiram Percy Maxim?"

I thought a long time. I did not know how to answer. I felt anything I might guess would be away off the mark, so I replied I could not think how old he might be, but "he must be awful old."

"Well, I am sixty-three years old," he replied, smiling. He was leaning against a rail fence as he said this and I was standing beside him, looking up into his face. He was a tall man as I remember him, and as we two of the same blood stood there looking at each other and discussing our respective ages, we must have made an interesting picture. He had his life behind him, while I had mine before me.

Not long ago my grandson, John Maxim Lee, aged six, and I were out walking and we fell to discussing ages. When I told him I was sixty-three, the same age that my grandfather was when he and I discussed ages, I could see that it was a figure just as far beyond his powers of comprehension as it had been to me. That picture of the past, when I was the uncomprehending little boy, floated before my mind. The tables had been turned. The little boy of long ago was now the grandfather, with his life behind him, and a new little boy had come into being, with his life all ahead of him. Thus do the generations of us men succeed one another.

My grandmother was a very remarkable person. She was quite short, probably not over five feet, had a sturdy and muscular little body, and had gray ringlets all over her head, steely blue eyes and the same intense, piercing gaze my sister Florence has at times. Her maiden name had been Harriet Boston Stevens; she was a daughter of "Old Brimstone Stevens," as he was termed in his day, on account of his firm belief in the efficacy of hell fire and brimstone. From what I have heard said, Old Brimstone Stevens must have been a very fearsome sort of person. Certainly, he seems to have instilled into the Maxim boys a generous supply of the fear of God and of himself, no small thing to accomplish.

The country in which these grandparents had grown up was the southern border of what are yet the wild lands of Maine. When my father was born they were living near a little grist mill some two or three miles out of Sangerville. Sangerville is some forty miles from Moosehead Lake. No spot on the face of this earth appeals to me quite so strongly as these Maine woods. Whether it is something inherited from my early ancestors, who did their part in beating back this wilderness, I do not presume to say; but when vacation time comes I think first of the Maine woods. They represent the last of the extensive and unsettled wild area in New England.

§2

My grandfather used to make an attempt to convey to me, a child of the city, the self-reliance which children of my father's day were compelled to exercise. He cited as an example my uncle Henry, whom I never saw, he having died before I was born. He said Henry, when a little boy of six, came into the house one day, crying lustily and nursing a wound on his leg. My grandfather asked him how he had hurt his leg. Henry replied the gander had bitten him. "Oh," said my grandfather, "don't bother me with a little matter like that. Go out and bite the gander in return."

This impressed Henry as being an excellent idea. The more he nursed his wounded leg and his wrath, the better the idea appeared. He finally decided to act. Returning outdoors, he hunted up the geese, selected the gander which had bitten him, and attacked him. A rough-and-tumble fight ensued which continued for a considerable time, the gander being about as strong as the boy. Boy and gander flopped around so much and fought so savagely that the geese began cackling, raising such a disturbance my grandfather was led to investigate. When he arrived upon the scene the fight was about over. Henry had the gander down and lay on top of him with his teeth set in the gander's neck. When my grandfather pulled the child off, the gander gave a few flaps and expired. Henry had killed him!

On another occasion, this time at Abbot Village, the dog belonging to the man who ran the general store became involved in a controversy with Henry. The dog was a mongrel, weighed some forty pounds, and had an unsavory reputation; he was an ugly brute and had bitten several persons. When he and Henry Maxim crossed swords he bit Henry. The dog did not know it at the time, but when he bit Henry Maxim he bit the wrong person. Henry flew into a passion and made after the dog. The latter retreated and Henry chased him.

The general store had no cellar, being built upon posts, which left a space underneath some three feet high. The dog ran into the space under the store. Nothing daunted, Henry followed him. Somewhere away in underneath, the dog turned on Henry. Henry grappled with him forthwith. What actually went on no one knows; but the people in the store at the time said the noise and the bumpings against the floor and the growls and snarls were fearful. The owner went out and peered under the store and shouted, but he said there was so much dust being kicked up and so much noise that he could see nothing and his voice could not be heard.

After a time the noise ceased and Henry crawled out from under the store. His clothing was in ribbons and he was covered from head to foot with dirt and blood. As he started for the river bank to clean up, he remarked to the bystanders, "That dog will never bite anybody again." In a space three feet high, in among the rocks and dirt, Henry had fought and killed a forty-pound dog barehanded!

My grandmother used to tell me about a scene they had with Henry when he was very little, probably about three and a half years of age. She and my grandfather were giving one of those country parties in the late fall, at which the neighbors are invited in to shuck corn, put up preserves, play games, and eat prodigious quantities of cookies, cakes, and pies. Henry in his bed upstairs was awakened by the noise and began to cry. My grandmother went up to quiet him. Instead of quieting him she made him cry louder. She was gone such a long time, and Henry was making so much noise, that my grandfather went up to lend a hand. He spanked Henry, in an effort to bring the child to his senses and stop crying. Instead of stopping, Henry started screaming. He had got out of hand completely.

There was a hogshead outside which caught the rain water from the roof. It being late in the fall, the water in this hogshead had a skim of ice over it. My grandfather, desperate over the disturbance and the interruption to the festivities, decided that severe measures were called for. Taking Henry from his bed, he carried him downstairs, strode with the screaming, kicking child through the assembled guests to the kitchen and thence to the hogshead, and plunged the child through the ice into the cold water. Of course, this quieted the child thoroughly. He was taken back upstairs, dried, and put back into bed. My grandfather and grandmother then joined their waiting guests.

No sooner had they returned than Henry, having regained his breath, and realizing what had been done to him and how angry he was, began screaming louder than ever. There was no use trying to run a party in all that noise, so my grandfather went upstairs a second time, brought the child down, and plunged him into the ice water again. Again it knocked out the last bit of breath the child had and he was quieted. Again he was returned to his bed and again an attempt was made to continue the party, although my grandmother said it was under considerable of a cloud.

While efforts were being made to reorganize the festivities Henry got his breath back, remembered how angry he was, and resumed his ear-splitting screams. By this time he was mad all the way through. My grandfather, now very determined, went upstairs, brought the screaming, kicking youngster down, plunged him into the ice water and *held him under* as long as he dared and not drown him. Naturally, the child stopped crying. He was put back in his bed and a third attempt was made to reorganize the party. Games were resumed, but the enthusiasm had been quenched, as the family conflict had damped everybody's spirit. While they were doing their best to live the difficulty down, Henry was heard again. This time there was nothing to do but call the party off and send the guests home. Henry screamed himself into exhaustion in a couple of hours and then fell asleep.

When Henry grew up he went into the Civil War— precisely the place for him, one would think. But by the irony of fate he fell ill, was invalided home, and died in bed.

§ 3

In due course the day came when I was to start for home. I had finished my breakfast and Uncle Sam had brought the horse and buggy to the door, when I discovered that I could not get my shoes on. I had not had them on for some five weeks and I suppose my feet had both grown and spread.

I called for my energetic little grandmother and told her my shoes were too small.

"Land sakes! Can't you get 'em on?" she ejaculated, realizing in a flash that after five weeks this easily might be true.

"No, Grandma, I can't. See! I can't even get my foot started in."

This was a pretty how-d'do! Everything had been thought of and made ready but this one thing. The buggy was waiting, Uncle Sam was urging us to hurry, and here we were at a standstill because I could not get my shoes on! Visions of going home barefoot floated across my mind and I suggested the idea; but my grandmother would not listen to it for an instant. She went down on her knees on the floor and in her characteristic way tried to force my foot in. To all appearances my foot was four or five sizes larger than my shoes. In desperation she got up, dashed to the door, and screamed to Uncle Sam that Hiram Percy Maxim could not get his shoes on. She waved her arms wildly to emphasize the seriousness of the situation. Normal persons would have called to each other and have sat down calmly and worked the problem out. Not so the Maxims. Anything of this order precipitated a panic or a riot, and all concerned became immediately and desperately excited.

Uncle Sam hopped down out of the buggy and came running. He had not understood what had been said and he had a perfectly good right to expect to find the house had caught fire, by the way my grandmother had acted. As he dashed into the room, his eyes snapping, he glared around wildly and shouted, "What's wrong, Marm?"

She had not been idle while he had been coming, having returned to the struggle with renewed energy. On her knees on the floor she was wrestling with might and main to get one of my feet into its shoe. "Can't get his shoes on!" she said between her teeth as she struggled. Without pausing a second, Uncle Sam flung himself into the fray. He grabbed my other foot and a shoe and began operations on his own account. One would have thought unless the shoes were got on me in the next sixty seconds the world surely would come to an end. Between the frantic pushing and pulling of both of them I was sliding all over the floor. I finally caught hold of the leg of the table to keep my position.

After a few vigorous attempts Uncle Sam dropped everything and dashed out into the kitchen. In a moment he returned with a cup containing flour and also with a tin plate. Snatching my shoe, and shouting to my grandmother, "Hold on a minute, Marm," he poured some of the flour into the shoe, shook it around vigorously, and emptied it out into the tin plate. Grabbing my foot, he started working it into the shoe and finally succeeded. Repeating the operation with the other shoe, he managed to get it on also. They were terribly tight and I assured the assembled relatives I could not walk a step; but the shoes were on, and whether or not I could walk in them was a minor matter.

§ 4

About this time I sat in on my first business conference. It was the practice of my father and mother to have a Mr. Spencer D. Schuyler and Mrs. Schuyler to dinner in Brooklyn on Sunday once in a while. Mr. Schuyler was either the president or some high officer in the United States Electric Lighting Company. My father was chief engineer, or something like it. Hartley and Graham, an old New York firm, which the older generation will remember, had some connection with the company, probably a financial one. Hartley and Graham were also owners of the Union Metallic Cartridge Company of Bridgeport, Connecticut. It appears that an arrangement of some kind was made, under the terms of which Hartley and Graham furnished factory space and capital for the development work which Messrs. Schuyler and Maxim had in mind in connection with their electric-light project.

At one of the dinners for the Schuylers at our house on Union Street, the two men remained at table after the ladies retired to the reception-room. I had become interested in their conversation, and, being a man, albeit a small one, I remained with the other men, listening to every word they uttered and watching the way Mr. Schuyler smoked his cigar. My father never smoked, so smoking was something of a novelty to me. Mr. Schuyler was a business executive and knew very little about electrical matters. My father seemed to be on the defensive most of the time with him, explaining that there were technical limitations beyond which it was impossible to go, even if the promised reward were great; but Mr. Schuyler chafed at these limitations, pointing out the opportunities that were offered if certain things could be done. After a lengthy conference, Mr. Schuyler became prophetic. Said he, "Maxim, you may say what you like, but I can see the day coming when electricity will be generated in large electricity works and be distributed through the streets for house lighting just as gas is generated in large gasworks today and distributed through the streets for house lighting."

To this my father shook his head and replied, "No,

Schuyler. You are looking too far ahead. Such a day may come; but there are too many unsolved technical problems for me to believe it will be in our times."

I fancy this particular conversation must have occurred in 1878 or 1879. The electric arc lamp had just about emerged from the experimental stage. It gave the most wonderful artificial light the world had ever seen. It was such an advance over the only other artificial light available, the gas jet, that a great business opportunity was foreseen by those interested. But the arc lamp was too hot and too bright and too large for many purposes, so that a race began between Edison and Maxim to see which would be first with an incandescent electric lamp. This incandescent development work seems to have been undertaken on a large scale after Schuyler and Maxim had succeeded in interesting Hartley and Graham. I have one of my father's old diaries. It is for the year 1880 and it is in as good condition as when he carried it around in his pocket. It had what he used to call a Russia-leather binding, which had a characteristic odor. I remember when I used to climb up on him I could smell this Russia leather. The diary has a trace of this odor today. It is a beautiful piece of work, this old notebook, has his name and address embossed in gold on it, and must have cost him a pretty penny.

Under the date of January 1, 1880, in my father's handwriting, appears this entry:

At home in Brooklyn all day. Write to Schuyler relating to the Edison light question.

The next day, January 2, 1880, he wrote:

Call on Hartley. See Schuyler. This day we commence in dead earnest the experiments so long delayed on the electric light in a vacuum space. Apparatus for experiment ordered. Go to Pearl River and get from old man B—— a lamp made one year ago. Satisfaction.

This reference, "light in a vacuum space," makes it appear the incandescent electric lamp was not yet an actuality. The reference to a lamp being made at Pearl River a year previously indicates to me that he built one experimental lamp there, and I imagine that the early arc lamp development work was done there. I remember being taken to Pearl River, New Jersey, when a child. There was a factory there and I remember a lecture given in this factory by my father in which he demonstrated several electrical phenomena, and also a very powerful electric arc searchlight.

An entry under the date of January 3, 1880, reads:

In New York, purchasing apparatus for electric light. Hunting up a glass blower. Go to Bridgeport in the evening.

An entry on January 6, 1880, reads:

Make drawings of current regulator. Prepare case for patent office. Application 1878.

This suggests that he had something in the way of an application in the Patent Office in 1878.

On January 9, 1880, he wrote:

Room finished complete. But no glass blower comes.

This glass-blower and the glass vacuum pump he was to make gave him plenty of trouble, evidently, for all through the diary are entries indicating his desperation over the glass-blowers and the pump. For example, on January 10, 1880, there appears this entry:

Ready for glass blower but he cometh not. Whooping cough worse.

I remember very vividly this whooping-cough trouble. He would have a spasm at home in the evening and cough and whoop and turn purple in the face, driving my mother to the verge of distraction. His habit, when he felt the cough coming, was to hurry to a doorway, put out both arms and brace himself between the sides of the doorway and then *cough* and *cough*! I used to fear he might explode. After a spasm had passed he would be very cross and watery-eyed.

Succeeding entries suggest the progress he was making.

On January 14, 1880:

Glass blower comes. Contract for pump. Sterling on rheostat. Determine to make a wheel commutator with a surface a la friction gearing. Sterling approves of it. Work in evening on regulator.

On January 29:

Oh the pump. Boss nuisance. Glass blower fooling with pump.

On the next day the entry reads simply:

Oh the *pump*!

On February 2:

No glass blowers. Start up my regulator. All right. A big thing.

On February 5:

My 40th birthday. Work on lamps all day. Lecture in evening on Electricity at Opera House.

On February 7:

Pump finished and one lamp finished. Machine, lamp and regulator all working first time in the world. Gasoline an apparent success.

On March 10:

Mr. S. D. Schuyler visits shop and sees incandescent lamps. Says to me, "Maxim, light a house in New York with those lamps and I'll sell your stock for 200 cents on the dollar."

In the early days of the development work on the incandescent electric lamp, Mr. Schuyler and my father had offices in the old Equitable Building at 120 Broadway in New York. These offices were taken over by the United States Electric Lighting Company when the latter company was ready to sell electric-lighting equipment. These old offices were destined to remain electric-light offices for many years, for when the electric-light industry became established and the modern Westinghouse Electric and Manufacturing Company became the final owners of the United States Company, they maintained the old office at 120 Broadway. I am informed that my father's picture hung on the wall there until the old building burned in recent times.

As a little boy I can remember the troublesome glass-blowers at work in the old Equitable Building. One of them, by the name of Pflock, made a marvelous glass pipe for me one day, as my father and I watched him. Demonstrations of the wonderful new electric light were given frequently. One of these demonstrations was to immerse an incandescent lamp in a glass jar full of water and watch it "burn" under water. This would not attract passing notice today; but in those days it

[164]

was considered marvelous, because a gas light would not burn under water. People came from far and near to see the unbelievable sight. Later on the company established a factory in the vicinity of Twenty-fifth Street and Avenue B in New York. In this factory the company made a real start in the electric-light business. I used to visit it frequently and came to know many of the leading men. There are a few of them left who never fail to tell me they remember me from the days when I was a little boy and my father used to bring me to the factory.

Both Mr. Schuyler and my father lived to see the day when Mr. Schuyler's prophecies came true a thousand times over.

§ 5

At about the time of which I am writing my father bought a twenty-one-foot steam-launch. She was a thing of beauty, with all her polished and nickel-plated work. He named her the *Flirt*. I quickly learned about steam-engines and steam-boilers, and what must be done and what must not be done with them. We used to cruise around New York Bay.

My mother despised the *Flirt*, as she did all craft excepting ferry-boats. She went with us only infrequently. Invariably she was badly frightened and sea-sick. One day she became so frightened and so ill that my father had to put her ashore at Staten Island so that she could go home on the ferry-boat.

On one occasion, my father had me go aboard the *Flirt* immediately after school, build a fire under the boiler, get up steam, and have everything all shipshape for him at five o'clock, when he was to arrive with another gentleman. At five o'clock I had steam up and everything in order. When he and his friend arrived, I noticed that the latter had to be led down the float to our boat. Clearly he was blind. Arrived alongside, my father guiding him, he put one foot out and felt the boat. After forming an idea as to her size, he came aboard, my father assisting him. He sat down, felt of the seats, got the general layout of the cockpit, and finally moved down toward the stern. Then he asked to be told about the engine and boiler. Before starting to explain them my father beckoned me over. Putting my hand in that of the blind gentleman's he said, "Mr. Herreshoff, this is my son Hiram Percy Maxim."

Then turning to me he said, "Percy, this is Mr. Herreshoff, who knows more about boats than any other man in the world."

Mr. Herreshoff took my hand and held it in his and smiled a very lovely smile. He felt of my head, evidently estimating my height. He said he always liked to meet little boys and asked me how old I was. I told him, and he drew me to a seat close beside him, put his arm around me and asked my father to continue. While my father explained the power plant, this kindly gentleman kept his arm around me. I recall that he kept saying, as my father explained detail after detail, "I see. I see." I thought this a curious remark in view of the fact that he was stone blind. This gentleman was Mr. John B. Herreshoff, one of the founders of the famous boat-building company which is still in business at Bristol, Rhode Island. Mr. Herreshoff long since passed on.

After I had become familiar with the steam-plant on the *Flirt* I wanted to know about other steam-plants. The first to receive my attention was the railroad locomotive. I must have driven my father desperate with my questions about steam-locomotives.

This obsession of mine reached such a stage that he appealed to my mother. "Good Lord!" said he. "Is there no way we can satisfy this boy's thirst for information about steam-locomotives?"

"I think if he were allowed to see a real one it might satisfy him," said she.

So it was arranged that I should be taken to one of the terminal stations of the new Sixth Avenue Elevated Railroad in New York, where James, who had been

our man at Fanwood, was engineer of one of the locomotives.

In those days there were only three methods of propelling railroad cars—by horses, by endless cable, and
by steam. The elevated lines in New York were operated
by little steam locomotives. And thus it came I was
taken uptown somewhere in New York and shown one
of these little locomotives. I was but moderately impressed. These locomotives were small, they had no
tender at all, everything about them was all bunched
together, and they did not even have a bell. They were
so malformed, it seemed to me, that unless one were
told one would hardly suspect they were locomotives
at all.

James helped me into the cab of the one of which
he was the engineer, and then he ran it out of the shed
for a few yards and backed it in again. He explained
how it was operated, and the differences between the
way matters were arranged on a locomotive and on a
boat. I saw the principles were the same, but the application of these principles was startlingly different.

When I returned home my father asked me if I
were satisfied now that I had had a good look at a locomotive. To his consternation I was worse than ever.
Having seen the inside of an imitation locomotive, I
could not rest until I saw the inside of a real one. I

probably made everybody's life utterly miserable, for when the locomotive complex fastened itself upon me I talked locomotive all the time and made every effort to have the other members of the family do the same.

My mother and father and I were invited to spend a Sunday at Paterson, New Jersey, visiting friends, and they decided that this trip would offer an opportunity for me to see a real locomotive. They accordingly made arrangements to have me ride out to Paterson in the cab of the locomotive of our train.

When we walked out on the platform of the railroad station at Hoboken, I with my hand in my father's, while my mother went into one of the passenger-cars, I began to have misgivings. The enterprise was assuming more serious proportions than I had contemplated. Arrived at the great, black, hissing monster, my courage began to ooze away. But a hard experience with my father in the past had taught me there must be no backing out. I positively must go through with the business even though it killed me. And so, after a word with the engineer, who was leaning out of his cab window and looking very grimy and dirty, my father lifted me up and the engineer helped me into the seat in front of him. I was completely overcome by the hissing noise. The engineer yelled something in my ear which I could not understand because of the hissing, but I recognized it as being intended as a kindly overture of some sort. His voice was the harshest and most rasping I had ever heard in all my life. I supposed that it had to be this way in order to penetrate the awful noise in which he lived. I was not very communicative by force of circumstances, even had I wished to be, which I did not, for I was too stunned by the awfulness of everything. Steam seemed to be hissing savagely to get out and threatening destruction to all concerned if it were much longer denied; everything seemed to be sizzling hot; something very close at hand was throbbing passionately; there was coal spilled over the floor, which was of steel; the fireman on the opposite side of the cab had a very dirty face and seemed not of this earth; and the engineer seemed to be deeply concerned about something back of us, for he kept peering out behind.

The heat was frightful and the smell of hot oil was sickening. While I was wondering why I ever came to such an inferno the engineer gave a violent jerk, convincing me that an emergency of some kind had suddenly arisen. He yelled something to the fireman, and then reached up and pulled with all his might on a long lever. The fireman snatched at a rope which he began to pull at regular intervals and which led me to suspect that he was ringing the bell. A fearful and terrible straining sound developed and I realized we were beginning to move. Then something underneath broke, or appeared to. The entire engine gave a fearful wrench and began coughing and snorting like an enraged monster; great clouds of steam and smoke belched from the smokestack, while the engine made a valiant effort to shake itself to pieces, trembling and vibrating in a manner calculated to raise every hair on my head. Something underneath was grinding as I never imagined anything in this world could grind. I glanced quickly at the engineer to see what he thought of the situation. Catching my eye, he smiled a reassuring smile and made a whirling action with his hand, pointing down, which I recognized meant that the driving wheels were slipping on the rails. My immediate fears were allayed, but I was a long way from being at ease in my mind.

We ran along over a maze of switches and cross tracks which caused me to marvel at the confidence of the engineer that his beast of an engine would take these switches and not run off the track. He did not seem to concern himself enough to watch out ahead and see where he was going. In a few minutes, and with no warning of any kind, we plunged headlong into a tunnel. We came upon it so suddenly, what with all the curves and switches, it made me flinch. I expected we were going to run headlong into the masonry which framed the tunnel entrance.

The moment we entered the tunnel a new complication arose. This one defied any explanation I could bring to bear. I was face to face with the most baffling mystery I had encountered in all my short life. It was so baffling as to cause me to forget the deafening noise, the frightful jolting, the heat, smell, fire, smoke, and hissing steam. It was dark in the tunnel. Right straight ahead of us there seemed to be something like a bird-house on the top of a high shiny pole. My first impulse was to dodge, as it seemed unavoidable that we should hit it. Strange to say, however, we could not seem to reach it; and yet there it stood directly in front of us. I could see that the bottom of the shiny pole was very close to the front of the engine. I cudgeled my brains, struggling to account for it. For the first time in my life my eyes were deceiving me.

I suppose I stared at that bird-house on the top of the shiny pole for two minutes before it resolved itself into the outlet portal of the tunnel and the glistening steel rails leading to it. I was so impressed and upset by this optical illusion that I could not adjust myself to what was real.

Every once in a while the fireman seemed to encounter some new and terrible emergency. With no warning, he would leap from his seat, grab something and pull desperately at it, and there usually would follow some kind of an ear-splitting clang. The fire door would burst open, an inferno of flame would be disclosed within the firebox; the fireman would peer into this inferno and seem to consider diving into it in order to fix something. But he would always think of another expedient, whereupon he would dash for the tender and engage in mortal combat with some kind of a long article which I could not see. Then he would attack the fire savagely with another long tool which he would withdraw smoking hot. He would slam this long hot tool down on the steel floor and dash out into the tender again, be gone for some seconds, and then dash back and proceed to shovel coal into the fire feverishly. He did this shoveling in such desperation that I was convinced he was doing his utmost to save all our lives. The shoveling done, he would slam the fire door shut, pitch the shovel into the tender, and scramble for his seat as though the devil himself were after him, and then gaze idly out his window and wave to somebody, appearing utterly to forget the emergency he had been fighting. To a little boy this exhibition was bewildering.

The engineer was less excitable. However, he made me very nervous, for he could not seem to resist the temptation to keep adjusting handles. A new and more alarming noise developed every time he touched one. The engine itself seemed to me to be bent upon its own destruction. It appeared to be rapidly coming to pieces, crashing and pounding and reeling drunkenly in its headlong plunge down the track. I could not but feel that if we arrived safely in Paterson it would be a marvelous achievement; and under no circumstances could I imagine anyone having the courage to start out again with this clattering, drunken, wheezing machine, once it got us safely to our destination.

In due course we staggered into the station at Paterson and the engineer was successful in stopping the dreadful monster at the right place without killing anybody. My father came up in a few moments, thanked the engineer, and lifted me down.

"Well, Percy, how did you like it?" he inquired as we walked back to join my mother. My ears were ringing with the noise and I was half stunned, but I answered, "Not very much."

After this I pursued the subject of locomotives with my father whenever a favorable opportunity offered, but not with that burning passion which had previously possessed me.

§ 6

One day I saw in Crandall's toy-store on Fulton Street a small stationary steam-engine. It was a little bit of a thing, having a copper boiler which would hold not more than a quarter of a teacup of water. It had a diminutive alcohol lamp under the boiler and a single oscillating engine on top of the boiler. It was a very primitive sort of a steam-engine, but it was real and it would run by steam. When my father came home that evening I told him of what I had seen.

"Gosh, Papa, you ought to see it! It has a little fly-wheel and all!" I told him.

My enthusiasm was so overpowering that he put down his paper and looked at me, with that quizzical expression in his face which made him look as though he were trying not to laugh.

"Oh, I've seen those engines. They stand up, don't they? It's an upright design. And the engine has a lead flywheel on one end of its shaft and a grooved pulley on the other end. Is that right?"

"Yes, that's right. Gee, Papa, but couldn't we have fun if we had one!"

"Do you know what the grooved pulley is for?" he asked.

I did, for I had seen a larger engine of this type driving a lot of things which looked like machines in a little toy factory.

"Yes. I know what that's for. You put a string on it and run the string to another wheel and it makes the other wheel go. They have a little toy factory down at Crandall's and all the machines are made to go by strings and wheels from one engine. Gosh, Papa! You ought to go down to Crandall's and see all the things they have."

"Is it open at night, do you suppose?" asked my father, still with that quizzical look.

"I don't know whether they are open at night. Wait till I ask Mamma," and I was off like a wild thing for my mother upstairs.

"Mamma, do you suppose Crandall's is open at night?"

"Crandall's?"

"Yes. You know. Crandall's toy-store, downtown."

"Oh! No, I don't think so, except on Saturday nights."

Hurrying back downstairs, I told him Mamma thought they were open at night only on Saturdays. He had returned to his paper during my absence, and all I could get out of him was that he would go down some Saturday evening and look at the engines.

When Saturday evening came I was on his trail and he happened to be in the mood, so he and I set out for Crandall's. I was so excited I could not walk; I had to skip and jump. Arrived at Crandall's, I pointed out the engine in the show window and he took a good look at it.

"Let's go inside and see what it's like," he finally remarked. Things were coming along beautifully. I never had induced him to go into a store that he did not buy me something before he got out.

A young woman waited upon us and my father told her we had come in to look over their steam-engines. She knew her business, for she brought out samples of every steam-engine they had in the store.

My father, the chief engineer of the United States Electric Lighting Company, pleaded ignorance of machinery, and he quickly had the young lady so completely tangled up with his questions that I had to step in and prompt her. She was not at all well informed about steam-machinery. When I explained a detail to her I recall that she and my father exchanged glances and smiles. It was not very long before I found myself explaining the engines to both of them, pointing out how they were made ready for a start and how they were operated after steam was up. My father appeared to be intensely interested but particularly stupid.

"Do you have to bother with putting water in it to make it go?" he would ask. I was too excited to realize that I was being led on.

"You have to have water to boil if you are going to get any steam, Papa. You have to have water in the *Flirt's* boiler, don't you?"

"The *Flirt* is our steam-launch," my father felt called upon to explain to the saleswoman. Then to me: "Oh yes. But the *Flirt* is a steam*boat.*"

I thought this about as weak an argument as could be devised. I was surprised that his knowledge should be so superficial.

"Steam*BOAT!*" I exploded. "What's that got to do with it, Papa? It's the steam-engine *in* the boat that makes the boat go. The steam is for the engine—not the boat," and I shot him a sharp look of impatience.

"Oh!" he answered uncomprehendingly.

"Did you think the steam pushed against the boat and made it go?" I asked, becoming exasperated and eyeing him intently.

"Well—I— Something pushes against the boat, Percy, or it wouldn't go."

"Gosh, Papa! I thought you knew more than that. Look here. To get steam you have to boil water, don't you?"

"Yes."

"When you boil water and get steam you let the steam go into a steam-engine, don't you?"

"Yes."

"When you let steam into a steam-engine it makes the engine go, doesn't it?"

"Yes."

"When the steam-engine goes it makes the propeller go, doesn't it?"

"Yes—but ——"

"But what?"

"It seems— I should think— Never mind. Go ahead."

"Well, when the propeller goes, it pushes against the water and this makes the boat go ahead. Everybody knows that, Papa."

By this time I suppose my eyes were flashing and my voice had become very loud and penetrating, for I remember that we were the center of all eyes in the store.

"That's all right if you have a boat; but this is not a boat," my father insisted, picking up the smallest of the engines, idly twisting the little flywheel and looking very silly.

"Of course it's not a boat. It's an engine, Papa. But it will go if you put water in the boiler and light the lamp. Anyway, I can make it go."

"Are you sure you can make it go, Percy?"

"Yes, Papa, I'm sure."

"Who told you how to make it go?"

"Mr. Haynes bought me a little steamboat when I went to his house in Boston that time I went to Wayne alone, and it had a little engine in it something like this one. And anyway, I know about these engines."

At this point he nodded to the saleswoman and she wrapped the engine up and handed it to me. When we had it at home I found, to my surprise, that my father knew more about the engine than I did. He explained the penalty when too much water is put into the boiler, or too little water, and for failure to blow out the lamp before the last bit of water is boiled away.

I played with this engine for a long time, learning its tricks, its good points and its bad points and every minute detail of its construction. I must have impressed my parents with my genuine love and appreciation of it, because the day came when my father bought me a little steam-locomotive, train of cars, and track. I was overcome! My father explained to me how the engine was constructed and how it had to be operated, emphasizing that it was a very expensive toy, was a real steam railroad in miniature, and that failure to handle it carefully and intelligently would quickly ruin it beyond repair.

That evening he and I set up the track, got up steam, and ran the outfit. It was wonderful! I suppose this was the high point in my life up to this time. I actually owned my own steam-locomotive and railroad! I am glad to be able to say I was as good as my word, for I played regularly with this little steam-train for many years, and never injured the boiler or any of the delicate machinery.

Some twenty-nine years after my father gave me this
steam-train I gave my son one almost exactly like it.
He got the same exquisite pleasure from his that I did
from mine, and he did even better than I did, for while
he played regularly with his train for many years, it
is still in good running order today, though it must be
over twenty years old. My hope is that I may see the
day come when the second generation will be handed
this identical toy to play with.

§ 7

I recall what was to me a series of very impressive
evenings on my next visit to Wayne. (This time my
father accompanied me.) It seems to have been a custom of my grandfather's for Samuel to read aloud to
the family. When evening came and it was time to start
the reading aloud, my grandmother would take her seat
in a low rocking-chair and start knitting or sewing.
Beside her was a small table on which stood a kerosene-
lamp. My grandfather would sit in his large rocking-
chair in the center of the room, his hands folded in
his lap and his large dark eyes staring into space. He
rarely spoke.

Before a high desk on a high stool would sit my
uncle Sam, the reader. Another small kerosene-lamp
furnished him light. The remainder of the room would

[181]

be dark and mysterious to me, for I was accustomed to plenty of gaslight when evening came. On the floor near the reader, his back resting against the wall, would sit my uncle Hudson, known in the family as "Ike." Astride a chair and also close to the reader would sit my father. I sat in a small chair. I was careful to place this chair close to my grandmother's side. She was a woman and the nearest thing to a mother that was available to me. It seemed to me the better part of wisdom to be as near to her as possible.

On this visit the book being read was Mark Twain's *Roughing It.* Uncle Sam had a wonderful voice. It was deep and resonant and dramatic. His wavy, jet-black hair, his flashing dark eyes, and his remarkably handsome face suggested Wilkes Booth, the actor, my mother used to say. Hudson and my father were of the same type, both having wavy black hair and very dark eyes. When a passage was read which impressed these young men as humorous they would throw back their heads and laugh so loudly and savagely that it frightened me. The deep-throated voices, the reckless abandon, and the noise of their feet scuffling on the bare floor, seemed terribly sinister to me. When the end of the humorous passage was reached, Uncle Sam would add his roars to that of the others.

During these scenes my grandmother would never

look up from her work, except to look at me to see if I were awake or asleep, I suppose. My grandfather, likewise, would sit in silence, bolt upright in his chair, his hands folded in his lap, and never change the expression on his face. I have heard much reading in the days which have come since those early ones down in Maine; but never have I heard anything so dramatic, virile, and commanding.

My father and I returned to Brooklyn after a ten days' visit. Little did I realize, when I said good-by and drove away, that more than forty years were to pass before I should drive back over that road and that I was never again to see my grandfather and my grandmother. They died a few years after this. When next I drove down that road to the old house I had with me a wife, a fourteen-year-old son, and an eight-year-old daughter. I tried to convey to my children an idea of the place as it had been when I was last there with my father; but it was impossible. The old atmosphere had gone. All that was left was the old house and my uncle Sam, now an aged man with failing eyesight. It was the end of that particular generation of the house of Maxim.

PART V

MANY years ago, during one of my visits to Chicago, I met Judge Kohlsaat, then a conspicuous figure. After we had finished the business matters about which I had to consult him, he asked me if I were any relation to Sir Hiram Stevens Maxim. I told him I was his son. "Well," said he, "I have the greatest respect for your father's persistence. I was crossing the Atlantic not so long ago and he gave an exhibition of determination which I have rarely seen equaled.

"I was sitting in the dining-saloon of the steamer one day when a disheveled, white-haired old gentleman came in and sat down at a table. He was a distinguished-looking man with his bushy white hair; but he was in bad shape, for his clothing was terribly rumpled and he wore no collar and no necktie. He gave an order to the steward and it was evident to everyone that he was suffering from seasickness. The steward returned in a few minutes with a tureen of soup, which he placed before Sir Hiram, and from which he proceeded to ladle out a portion into a soup-plate. Sir Hiram went to extremes to avert his gaze from the soup while the steward was ladling it out. The ladling done, Sir Hiram picked up his napkin and looked intently at the soup in his plate, making no motion to eat it. Suddenly he clapped his napkin to his mouth, jumped to his feet, and beat a hasty retreat. Everybody smiled at his predicament and decided that he had had all the lunch he would care for that day.

"But," continued Judge Kohlsaat, "we had not estimated our man properly. In fifteen minutes he came striding back into the dining-saloon, looking very hollow-eyed and ill. Seating himself, and with determination written all over him, he said to the steward, 'Bring that soup in again.' The steward smiled and departed. In a few minutes he returned with another tureen of soup, and went through the same procedure of ladling it out. When he had served the soup the steward withdrew, watching to see what would happen, as did everyone else in the dining-saloon. The old gentleman picked up his spoon with great deliberation, very evidently fighting a royal battle with his insides. He toyed with the spoon a moment, finally putting it into the soup and slowly stirring it. Suddenly clapping his napkin to his mouth again, he jumped to his feet and again beat a hasty retreat out of the dining-saloon.

"Again everyone concluded that the old fellow was through for that meal. But to our amazement, in another fifteen minutes he came striding back into the saloon, looking, if possible, a little worse than before. He resumed his seat and ordered the steward to 'Bring in that soup once more.' Every eye was now on the old gentleman, for this had become a real sporting event. The steward brought the soup again and the same procedure of ladling it out was gone through with. Sir Hiram picked up his spoon, toyed with it a moment, placed it in the soup, stirred it around a few times, braced his shoulders, and lifted the spoonful of soup to his mouth. He got the soup into his mouth, but the instant it arrived there was a violent explosion and he had to grab his napkin and hasten out. We waited for him to return again, but he never came. He was a sick man; but in spite of it he had made three gallant attempts to eat his soup."

§ 2

Another example of my father's unusual tenacity was the way he followed up two sharpers who robbed him. The robbery occurred in Paris. In some sort of a transaction, the nature of which I never knew, he had to make payment in gold. The money was counted out on a table in an office on the second floor of a building on one of the principal streets of Paris. Immediately it was counted out, two strangers approached and one of them, with a deft motion, swept all of the money into an opened bag and ran for the street. The other man made as though to assist in the capture of the thief, but upset so many chairs, and created so much confusion, that my father's progress was delayed. By the time he could reach the street the thief had become lost in the crowds.

It was a considerable sum of money, and my father took the matter up immediately with the Paris police. He was stopping in London, where he had taken up residence, and had gone over to Paris for the purpose of completing this transaction, whatever it was. Several days of intensive effort were spent in Paris with the police, but no trace of the thief and his confederate could be found. He was forced to give up and return to London. Knowing him as I do, I can picture his mental attitude. He had been taken advantage of. So long as he lived his search for those who had victimized him would never cease. Thenceforward his eyes would search every group of men for those two sharpers.

Over six years rolled by and he was returning to London from Paris. At one of the stations in France on the way to the boat at Calais, he went into the railroad station for a cup of hot tea. A train bound for Paris was also in the station, and several people were standing round the stove, warming themselves. Looking them over, as was his invariable habit since he was robbed, he was electrified to recognize one of the men as one of those who had robbed him. Deciding there was no use in waiting for the police, he rushed up and tackled the man, shouting, *"Police! Police! Police!"* A savage fight began immediately. The other members of the group vanished as the two men struggled in the station, no one lending my father a hand, notwithstanding his call for police assistance. In the meantime the train for Paris departed. Immediately thereafter the train on which my father had been traveling started. The thief saw his last opportunity. Slipping out of his coat, he eluded my father's hold, dashed out of the station and down the platform, and caught and climbed on the last carriage.

Not to be diverted by this move, my father also dashed down the platform and managed to catch hold of the guard rail of this last carriage. Just as he did this the train entered a tunnel. The robber endeavored to kick Father in the face and thus beat him off the train; but in the darkness he did not succeed in landing a single kick. A woman seated in the last compartment of the carriage saw the fighting and screamed, and a guard pulled the signal cord, which brought the train to a stop in the tunnel. This was all my father could have desired. Getting hold of his man, he dragged him off the carriage down on to the ground in the tunnel, and there he beat him into subjection, possibly much as his brother handled the dog down in Maine.

The train crew quickly collected, and with their help the man was taken back to the railway station. My father is said never to have released his grip upon him, trusting no one but himself. The police of the town were called, my father's luggage was removed from the train, and he devoted himself exclusively to seeing to it that the man was properly locked up in the town jail. In the course of time he had him transferred to Paris. My father, running true to form, gave up his business for the time being, moved over to Paris, and devoted himself to securing the man's conviction. Weeks were necessary to collect the evidence, and considerable money had to be spent, but this was all gladly contributed in the effort to "get his man." The thief was finally sent to one of the French penal colonies for a long term of years.

Seven more years had rolled by when, one Thursday night in the Crystal Palace in London, my father believed he caught sight of his other man in a candy booth. When he was able to get to this booth the man had gone. He bought some candy and engaged in conversation with the young woman attendant, but did not succeed in obtaining any information of value. He waited around until the place closed for the night, but the man did not come back.

The next day he appealed to Scotland Yard. From the time the Crystal Palace opened in the afternoon until it closed at night several Scotland Yard detectives and my father kept the candy booth under surveillance. Their watch availed nothing on Friday. The exhibition was to close at midnight on Saturday. Nothing happened Saturday afternoon, and Saturday night, as the closing time approached my father became more and more disappointed. But just before midnight, when my father had given up hope, he caught sight of his man entering the candy booth. He gave a signal to the detectives and they descended upon the fellow and arrested him.

A long tedious procedure had then to be followed to extradite the prisoner to France and then to try him in Paris; but this was nothing to my father. He postponed all his business affairs and devoted himself exclusively to the job of convicting his man. After many weeks this man, too, was sent to the French penal colony.

Nothing I could recount would so well illustrate my father's character as this tireless search on his part for the two men who had robbed him. For thirteen years he searched every face for the men he sought. He never relinquished his intensity of purpose and never permitted himself to give up. It was this same spirit which had animated his brother Henry when he bit the gander to death and when he killed a forty-pound dog for biting him. They were the wrong persons to impose upon.

§ 3

In later years my father became a British subject. In consideration of the service his Maxim gun had been to British arms in the Sudan he was knighted by Queen Victoria and became Sir Hiram Stevens Maxim. In the course of events his machine-gun business was absorbed by Vickers Sons & Company and the firm became Vickers Sons and Maxim. It was one of the largest firms in England, building battleships and all that went into them. My father became internationally known and occupied a position of great importance and dignity.

At one time during the height of his glory it was observed by some of his associates that he went out every evening about seven-thirty and did not return until about nine-thirty. His associates had come to know him and his characteristics, and it was agreed that this mysterious absence every evening had better be investigated, lest Sir Hiram be led into doing something foolish and get himself into difficulties. And so he was trailed one evening and seen to enter a building in the business district of London. About nine o'clock he came out and returned home.

Investigation disclosed that he had hired a front room in the top of the building. When the room was searched the only things found were a chair, a long brass tube, and a bag of black beans. Had I been one of the investigators I would have solved the mystery the moment I saw the brass tube and the beans. It so happened that the Salvation Army paraded every evening in this part of London and held a meeting on the opposite side of the street. For some time complaints had been made to the police that some one was disturbing the Salvation Army group by dropping beans upon them. The beans always came from directly overhead and it was thought that some miscreant in the building in front of which the meetings were held was guilty of tossing out the beans. However, careful watch had failed to disclose anyone throwing beans, and a search of the building produced no evidence. Where the beans came from was an unsolved mystery.

Those who were trailing Sir Hiram kept a watch on the window of his room, and it was thought that he was seen at the window at times; but nothing was thought of this until some one picked up one of the beans which had been thrown at the Salvation Army and found it was the same kind of bean that Sir Hiram had in the bag in his room. That was enough. Sir Hiram was the bean-thrower. He was making use of the same trick he used when he was a young man and lived on Third Street in Brooklyn; he had been blowing the beans at the upper part of the building opposite, so that they bounced off and fell vertically, thus giving the impression that they were coming from directly overhead.

A session was held with Sir Hiram and it was explained that he had better give up this bean-blowing practice before he was discovered. He gave it up; but I know he had enjoyed himself mystifying the Salvation Army people and having all the blame laid at the door of the occupants across the street. The use of black beans should be noted. It was impossible to trace their flight in the dark.

And thus I come to the end of this intimate picture of that remarkable person, Hiram Stevens Maxim. I think it must be conceded that he was an unusual father, and that being his firstborn was an unusual experience. In this picture I have confined myself to his intimate family life. I have attempted to show that he had an extremely attractive side and also an extremely difficult one. He had a brilliancy which sparkled, a masterful cleverness and resourcefulness that placed him above any other man I ever knew. But he never quite learned how to be a father.